A Mediterranean Cookbook

A Collection of Persian, Lebanese,
and Turkish Recipes
(4th Edition)

By
BookSumo Press

Published by
http://www.booksumo.com

LEGAL NOTES

Table of Contents

Nutty Salted Pancakes

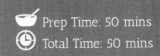

Prep Time: 50 mins
Total Time: 50 mins

Servings per Recipe: 1
Calories   70.3
Fat   4.4g
Cholesterol   45.6mg
Sodium   118.9mg
Carbohydrates   4.9g
Protein   3.3g

Ingredients

1 lb zucchini, trimmed and coarsely grated

2 C chopped green onions

4 eggs, beaten to blend

1/2 C all-purpose flour

1/3 C chopped fresh dill (or 1 1/2 T. dried dillweed)

1/3 C chopped fresh parsley

2 tbsp chopped fresh tarragon (or 2 t. dried)

1/2 tsp salt

1/2 tsp ground pepper

1/2 C crumbled feta cheese (about 3 oz.)

2/3 C chopped walnuts (about 3 oz.)

Olive oil

Directions

1. Transfer the zucchini to a fine mesh sieve and season it with some salt. Place it aside for 35 min then press it to remove the excess water.
2. Toss the zucchini, green onions, eggs, flour, chopped herbs, salt, and pepper in a large mixing bowl.
3. Grease a large skillet with some olive oil then use large tbsp to spoon the mix into the skillet in a round shape.
4. Cook the nutty pancakes for 3 to 4 min on each side or until they become golden brown then serve them with your favorite toppings.
5. Enjoy.

SAUCY GREENS
Potato Salad

Prep Time: 20 mins
Total Time: 45 mins

Servings per Recipe: 6
Calories	269.6
Fat	5.1g
Cholesterol	0.0mg
Sodium	238.9mg
Carbohydrates	52.4g
Protein	7.6g

Ingredients

3 onions cut into crescents

2 tbsp olive oil

1 1/2 lbs green beans

3 large ripe tomatoes cut into wedges

1 C tomato sauce

1 C water

3 large potatoes cut into chunks

Salt and pepper

Directions

1. Place a skillet over medium heat and heat the oil in it.
2. Cook in it the onions for 3 to 5 min or until it becomes golden.
3. Stir in the rest of the ingredients then put on the lid and let them cook for 5 to 10 min or until they become soft.
4. Serve your warm veggies salad with your favorite toppings.
5. Enjoy.

Peppery
Lamb Stew

Prep Time: 20 mins
Total Time: 2 hrs 10 mins

Servings per Recipe: 3
Calories   328.0
Fat   17.9g
Cholesterol   108.5mg
Sodium   170.5mg
Carbohydrates   5.6g
Protein   34.6g

Ingredients

1/2 kg boneless stewing lamb
2 tbsp olive oil
1 medium onion, finely chopped
1 garlic clove, minced
1/4 C chopped sweet pepper (red, orange, yellow, or green) (optional)
1/2 C canned tomatoes, pureed or 3/4 C chopped peeled tomatoes
3/4 C water

1/2 tsp baharat, spice mix Baharat Spice Blend or 1/2 tsp ground allspice
Salt
Fresh ground black pepper
1/4 C chopped parsley

Directions

1. Place a large pan over medium heat and heat in it half of the oil. Cook in it the lamb meat until it becomes evenly brown.
2. Drain it and place it aside. Add the rest of the oil and heat it. Sauté in it the onion, garlic and sweet pepper for 4 to 6 min. stir in the water with tomato.
3. Mix in the bahrat or allspice, salt and pepper to taste and most of the parsley.
4. Stir in the meat back then put on the lid and cook them for 1 h 30 min. once the stew sauce becomes thick, serve it hot with some rice.
5. Enjoy.

MINTY FETA
and Courgette Patties

🥣 Prep Time: 20 mins
🕐 Total Time: 45 mins

Servings per Recipe: 4
Calories	333.5
Fat	24.8g
Cholesterol	203.1mg
Sodium	624.3mg
Carbohydrates	14.6g
Protein	14.2g

Ingredients

1 large onion, chopped coarsely

3 tbsp sunflower oil

500 g courgettes, chopped finely

3 eggs

3 tbsp plain flour

2 sprigs of fresh mint, chopped

2 sprigs fresh dill, chopped

200 g feta cheese, mashed with a fork

Oil (for frying)

Directions

1. Place a large skillet over medium heat and heat 3 tbsp of oil in it. Cook in it the onion until it becomes golden and soft.

2. Stir in the courgettes and cook them until they are done.

3. Whisk the eggs with flour. Stir in the black pepper with herbs. Add the feta cheese and stir them gently followed by the onion and courgettes mix.

4. Grease a large skillet with some oil and heat it over medium heat.

5. Shape the mix into small patties using a tbsp then place them in the heated skillet. Cook them until they become golden brown on both sides.

6. Serve your courgette patties warm with your favorite toppings and enjoy.

Hot Lamb Kabobs
with Bloody Mary Hummus

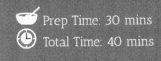 Prep Time: 30 mins

Total Time: 40 mins

Servings per Recipe: 2
Calories	648.4
Fat	45.3g
Cholesterol	117.2mg
Sodium	1111.9mg
Carbohydrates	23.5g
Protein	38.0g

Ingredients

350 g leg of lamb, fat trimmed

1 bell pepper, cut into chunks (any color)

1 red onion, half cut into chunks, half sliced

100 g white mushrooms

3 tbsp olive oil

1 cooked beetroot

75 g chickpeas, rinsed and drained (can)

1/2 lemon, juiced

1/2 tsp tahini

2 garlic cloves, crushed

1 tbsp harissa

1 tsp dried oregano

2 sprigs fresh rosemary, finely chopped

3/4 tsp himalayan pink salt

Directions

1. To make the kabobs: Cut the lamb meat into small dices.
2. Mix the sliced onion, 1 clove of garlic, harissa paste, oregano, rosemary and 1 tbsp of olive oil in a large mixing bowl to make the marinade.
3. Season the lamb pieces with some salt then stir them into the marinade. Place the kabobs in the fridge to marinate for 1 h.
4. To make the hummus:
5. Combine the beetroot, chickpeas, tahini, 2 tbsp of olive oil, 1/4 tsp salt, and 1 clove of garlic and lemon juice in a food processor then process until they become smooth.
6. Place the hummus aside until ready to serve.
7. Place the mushrooms with pieces of pepper, onion and lamb pieces into skewers.
8. Before you do anything preheat the grill and grease its grates. Cook in it the skewers for 3 to 5 min on each side. Once the time is up, serve your kabobs warm with hummus.
9. Enjoy.

MINTY
Beef Sandwiches

Prep Time: 10 mins
Total Time: 35 mins

Servings per Recipe: 4
Calories	206.4
Fat	3.9g
Cholesterol	13.4mg
Sodium	781.3mg
Carbohydrates	34.3g
Protein	7.7g

Ingredients

1 1/2 lbs lean ground beef
1/2 tsp salt
1/4 tsp pepper
1/4 tsp cumin
2 oz feta cheese, cut into 4 cubes
2 tbsp of fresh mint, chopped
4 pita breads (or 2 large ones cut in half)

Garnishing:

Hummus
Cucumber, thinly sliced
Red onion, thinly sliced
Fresh tomato, sliced
Fresh basil leaf
Fresh spinach leaves

Directions

1. Mix the beef, salt, pepper and cumin. Shape the mix into 4 pieces and place them aside.
2. Place the feta dices on a working surface and press them until they become flat then top them with the mint.
3. Flatten a piece of the beef mix on your hands slightly then place the feta piece in the middle then wrap the meat mix around it shaping it into a burger.
4. Repeat the process with the rest of the ingredients. Place a large skillet over medium heat and heat some oil in it.
5. Cook the patties in the hot pan for 6 to 8 min on each side. Once the time is up, serve your patties in the pita breads with your favorite toppings.
6. Enjoy.

Mediterranean
Omelets

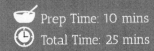 Prep Time: 10 mins

Total Time: 25 mins

Servings per Recipe: 4
Calories	243.5
Fat	11.9 g
Cholesterol	475.8mg
Sodium	184.4mg
Carbohydrates	18.2g
Protein	17.6g

Ingredients

9 eggs

200 g onions, sliced

1 bunch fresh parsley, chopped

300 g green peppers, diced

6 tomatoes, chopped

Butter, to taste

Salt, to taste

Directions

1. Beat the eggs in a mixing bowl. Season it with some salt.
2. Place a skillet over medium heat and melt the butter in it. Cook in it the pepper with onion, salt and tomato for 5 min.
3. Spread the veggies in the pan and pour the eggs all over them. Serve your omelets with the parsley on top and your favorite other toppings.
4. Enjoy.

LEMON FETA
Chicken Pizza

Prep Time: 20 mins
Total Time: 1 hr

Servings per Recipe: 6
Calories	265.9
Fat	11.1g
Cholesterol	75.2mg
Sodium	710.9mg
Carbohydrates	15.6g
Protein	28.6g

Ingredients

2 skinless chicken breasts
1/3 C lemon juice
1 tbsp olive oil
2 cloves garlic, crushed
1/3 C of fresh mint, chopped
1 medium onion, chopped

1 (425 g) cans crushed tomatoes
1 kg English spinach
2 Turkish bread (44cm)
200 g reduced fat feta cheese

Directions

1. Toss the chicken with lemon juice, oil, garlic and half the mint in a large mixing bowl. Place it in the fridge covered for 3 h.
2. Once the time is up, drain the chicken and place it aside then reserve the marinade aside.
3. Place a non-sticking pan of medium heat and heat it then brown in it the chicken breasts on both sides. Place them aside to lose heat for a while.
4. Cut the chicken breasts into slices. Pour the reserved marinade into the same pan and heat it.
5. Stir in the onion and cook it for 3 to 6 min or until it becomes soft.
6. Stir in the tomato and cook them for 12 min over low heat until the mix becomes thick.
7. Bring the mix to a boil. Steam or microwave the spinach until the soften and welt then press them with your hands to remove the excess water.
8. Place the Turkish bread on a lined up baking sheet spread on them the tomato mix followed by the chicken, spinach, feta and mint.
9. Preheat the oven. Cook in it the Turkish pizza for 22 min. serve them warm.
10. Enjoy.

Tzatziki
Steak Kabobs

Prep Time: 50 mins
Total Time: 1 day 50 mins

Servings per Recipe: 6
Calories   512 kcal
Fat   34.3 g
Carbohydrates   36g
Protein   15.7 g
Cholesterol   33 mg
Sodium   891 mg

Ingredients

Marinade:

2 large onions, chopped
2 garlic cloves, crushed
1/2 C olive oil
2 tbsp lemon juice
1 tsp dried oregano
1 tsp ground black pepper
1/2 tsp ground turmeric
1 pinch curry powder
1 tsp salt
1 lb beef flank steak, thinly sliced

Tzatziki Sauce:

8 oz sour cream
2 tbsp olive oil
1 tbsp lemon juice
1/2 tsp salt
1/2 tsp ground black pepper
1 tbsp chopped fresh dill
1 clove garlic, crushed
6 pita bread rounds

Directions

1. Put the onion in a mixing bowl then press it with a glass to get the excess water out from it.
2. add the 2 crushed garlic cloves, 1/2 C olive oil, 2 tbsp lemon juice, oregano, 1 tsp black pepper, turmeric, curry powder, and 1 tsp salt then combine them well.
3. Combine in the beef slices then put on a lid of a piece of plastic and place it in the fridge for 12 h.
4. Whisk the sour cream, 2 tbsp olive oil, 1 tbsp lemon juice, 1/2 tsp salt, 1/2 tsp black pepper, dill, and 1 crushed clove of garlic in a mixing bowl.
5. Cover it with a piece of plastic and place it in the fridge for 12 h to make the sauce.

6. Before you do anything preheat the oven broiler. Please the 6 rack inches away from the heat.

7. Drain the beef slices from the marinade and lay them on a greased baking sheet then season them with a pinch of salt.

8. Cook them in the oven for 6 min while flipping them halfway through time. Transfer the meat slices into the pita breads and top them with the cream sauce then serve them warm.

9. Enjoy.

Labneh
Lebanese Cream Cheese

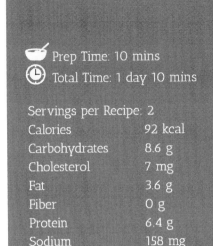

Prep Time: 10 mins
Total Time: 1 day 10 mins

Servings per Recipe: 2
Calories	92 kcal
Carbohydrates	8.6 g
Cholesterol	7 mg
Fat	3.6 g
Fiber	0 g
Protein	6.4 g
Sodium	158 mg

Ingredients

16 cups plain yogurt
1 tsp salt, or (your preferred amount)
1/4 cup olive oil

Directions

1. To make this recipe we will first need two things: some cheesecloth for lining a container (preferably a bowl) and a container. So grab these two things.
2. Now get your yogurt and put it into the cheesecloth lined dish. Also put in your salt with the yogurt.
3. Now a grab a colander and put it in the sink or into the dish to catch anything that drains off from the mixture.
4. Allow everything to drain for at least twenty four hours ideally.
5. What is left over from draining is our cheese.
6. Take the remaining contents and put them in another dish suitable for storage.
7. Combine with the cheese, some olive oil, making sure to mix it in well.
8. Make sure to put a lid on this container and keep it in the fridge.
9. Enjoy.

TURKISH PIZZAS
with Garlic Sauce

Prep Time: 2 hrs
Total Time: 1 day 4 hrs

Servings per Recipe: 10

Calories	480 kcal
Fat	20.1 g
Carbohydrates	57.6g
Protein	17.2 g
Cholesterol	35 mg
Sodium	571 mg

Ingredients

For the Lamb Sauce:

1 tsp chopped garlic

1 yellow onion, chopped

3 tbsp chopped fresh basil

1/2 C chopped fresh parsley

2 tbsp chopped fresh mint

1/2 tsp paprika

1/2 tsp ground cumin

1/2 tsp ground coriander seed

1/2 C green bell pepper, diced

1/2 C red bell pepper, diced

1/2 lemon, juiced

4 tsp olive oil

4 roma (plum) tomatoes, halved

1 lb lean ground lamb

6 tbsp double concentrated tomato paste

Cayenne pepper to taste

Salt to taste

For the Dough:

3 1/4 tsp active dry yeast

1/2 tsp white sugar

1 C warm water (110 degrees F/45 degrees C)

5 C all-purpose flour

2 tsp salt

1/4 C vegetable oil

1/2 C water

For the Garlic Sauce:

1 C plain yogurt

1/2 tsp chopped fresh parsley

1/4 tsp crushed garlic

Salt and ground black pepper to taste

For the Garnish:

1 C shredded green cabbage

1 C shredded red cabbage

Directions

1. Place a large pan over medium heat. Brown in it the lamb

2. Get a food processor: add to it the garlic, onion, basil, parsley, mint, paprika, cumin, coriander, diced bell peppers, lemon juice, tomatoes, and olive oil.

3. Process them until they become smooth. Stir in the tomato mix with tomato paste and

cook them for 16 min until they become thick while stirring all the time.

4. Add the pinch of salt with cayenne pepper and turn off the heat. Pour the mix into a casserole dish and place it aside to lose heat.

5. Cover it and place it in the fridge for 12 h.

6. Stir the sugar with yeast and 1 C of warm water. Mix the salt with flour in a large mixing bowl.

7. Stir the vegetable oil and 1/2 C water into the sugar and yeast water mix. Add the mix to the flour and mix them well with your hands.

8. Sprinkle some flour on a working surface and keep pulling it with your hands until it softens for 9 min.

9. Get a large bowl: grease it with some vegetable oil and place the dough on it. Cover it with a piece of plastic and place it aside to rise for 1 h.

10. Place the meaty tomato sauce aside to adjust to the kitchen temperature.

11. To make the creamy garlic sauce:

12. Stir the yogurt, parsley, crushed garlic, and salt and pepper. Place it in the fridge until ready to serve.

13. Before you do anything preheat the oven to 500 f.

14. Sprinkle some flour on a working surface and place the dough on it. Cut it into 10 pieces and roll each one into a circular shape.

15. Place the dough circles on a lined up baking sheet. Spread on each one of them the meaty tomato sauce. Cook the pizzas in the oven for 6 to 10 min until they become golden.

16. Place the pizzas on serving plates then top them with the garlic sauce and some shredded cabbage.

17. Enjoy.

Turkish Lamb and Beef Burgers

Prep Time: 30 mins
Total Time: 1 h 50 mins

Servings per Recipe: 6

Calories	381 kcal
Fat	25.1 g
Carbohydrates	9.9g
Protein	28.2 g
Cholesterol	142 mg
Sodium	548 mg

Ingredients

1 lb ground lamb

1 lb ground beef

1 tsp salt

1 tsp ground black pepper

1 tbsp ground cumin

2 tsp ground sweet paprika

3 tbsp tomato paste

2 onions, peeled and cut into chunks

4 cloves garlic, peeled

1 tbsp olive oil

1/4 bunch fresh parsley, chopped

3 tbsp all-purpose flour

2 small eggs

Directions

1. Place the lamb, beef, salt, pepper, cumin, paprika, and tomato paste in a large mixing bowl without combining them and put it aside.
2. Get a food processor: combine in the garlic with onion and process them while adding the olive oil gradually. Combine in the parsley and process them again.
3. Add the parsley mix to the meats mix and combine them well with your hands. Add the eggs with flour and mix them again with your hands. Place the mix aside to rest for 6 min.
4. Mix them again and shape the mix into several medium sized burgers. Place them on a baking sheet, cover them with a piece of plastic and place them in the fridge for 1 h.
5. Before you do anything preheat the oven broiler and put the rack 3 inches away from the heat.
6. Place the burgers on a foil lined up baking sheet and cook them in the oven until they become golden brown on both sides. Serve them warm with your favorite toppings.
7. Enjoy.

KARNIYARIK
Turkish Eggplants

🥣 Prep Time: 20 mins
🕐 Total Time: 2 hrs

Servings per Recipe: 6

Calories	288.3
Fat	10.9g
Cholesterol	44.4mg
Sodium	188.5mg
Carbohydrates	35.0g
Protein	18.1g

Ingredients

6 thin and long medium-size eggplants
Salt
Sunflower oil, for frying
2 onions, chopped
14 oz ground beef or 14 oz lamb
1 tbsp tomato paste
2 large tomatoes
1 tsp ground cinnamon
1/2 tsp ground allspice
Black pepper
1/3 C chopped flat leaf parsley
1 C tomato juice

Directions

1. Take of the eggplant caps while leaving the stems on then peel them by removing wide stripes leaving some of the skin in the process.
2. Fill a large bowl with water and 1 tbsp of salt then place in it the eggplants for 32 min.
3. Remove them from the water and pat them dry.
4. Place a large skillet over medium heat and heat some oil in it then cook it in the eggplants until they become slightly golden brown on each side.
5. Place another skillet over medium heat and heat 3 tbsp of oil in it. Add the onion and cook it for 4 min.
6. Stir in the meat and cook them for another 6 min. stir in the tomato paste with 1 chopped tomato, cinnamon, allspice, salt, pepper, and chopped parsley.
7. Cook them for 12 min over low heat while stirring all the time.
8. Before you do anything preheat the oven to 350 f.
9. Lay the browned eggplants in a greased casserole dish.
10. Use a sharp knife to make a slit in the belly of each eggplant without cutting completely then use a spoon to press it inside and make it hollow.
11. Spoon the meaty tomato mix into the slit of each eggplant then cut the remaining tomato into slices and places them on top.
12. Drizzle the tomato juice on top then place a piece of foil on top to cover them.
13. Cook the meaty eggplant casserole dish for 42 min then serve it warm.
14. Enjoy.

TURKISH
Chicken Kabobs

Prep Time: 20 mins
Total Time: 2 hrs 27 mins

Servings per Recipe: 4

Calories	539 kcal
Fat	32.5 g
Carbohydrates	8.4g
Protein	51.8 g
Cholesterol	186 mg
Sodium	1722 mg

Ingredients

1 C whole-milk Greek yogurt
2 tbsp freshly squeezed lemon juice, or more to taste
2 tbsp olive oil
2 tbsp ketchup
6 cloves garlic, minced
1 tbsp Aleppo red pepper flakes
1 tbsp kosher salt

1 1/2 tsp ground cumin
1 tsp freshly ground black pepper
1 tsp paprika
1/8 tsp ground cinnamon
2 1/2 lbs boneless, skinless chicken thighs, halved
4 long metal skewers

Directions

1. Get a mixing bowl: mix in it the yogurt, lemon juice, olive oil, ketchup, garlic, red pepper flakes, salt, cumin, black pepper, paprika, and cinnamon.
2. Stir in the chicken pieces into the mix. Put on a piece of plastic to cover them and place them in the fridge for 6 to 9 h.
3. Before you do anything preheat the grill and grease its grates. Grease the metal skewers.
4. Thread each chicken thigh into 2 skewers at the time horizontally. Cook the chicken kabobs for 4 to 5 min on each side then serve them.
5. Enjoy.

Tilapia Couscous Stew

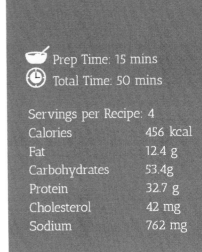

Prep Time: 15 mins
Total Time: 50 mins

Servings per Recipe: 4
Calories   456 kcal
Fat   12.4 g
Carbohydrates   53.4g
Protein   32.7 g
Cholesterol   42 mg
Sodium   762 mg

Ingredients

3 C water

1 1/2 C dry couscous

2 tbsp olive oil

1 small white onion, chopped

1 green bell pepper, chopped

2 cloves garlic, minced

1 C marinated artichoke hearts, liquid reserved

2 tsp capers, liquid reserved

12 small green olives

1 (14.5 oz) can chopped stewed tomatoes, drained

2 tbsp white wine (optional)

1 tbsp lemon juice

1 C water

2 tsp sumac powder

1 1/2 tsp crushed red pepper flakes

1 tsp dried basil

1 tsp cumin

1 tsp minced fresh ginger root

Ground black pepper to taste

1 lb tilapia fillets, cut into chunks

Directions

1. Get a saucepan: place it over medium heat and fill it with 3 C of water. Cook them until the start boiling. Add the couscous and put on the lid.
2. Turn off the heat and let it rest for 6 min.
3. Place a large pan over medium heat. Heat the oil in it. Cook in it the onion and green pepper for 6 min. add the garlic and cook them for an extra 3 min.
4. Stir in the artichoke hearts with reserved liquid, capers with reserved liquid, and olives, tomatoes, wine, lemon juice, and 1 C water.
5. Add a pinch of salt and sumac powder, red pepper, basil, cumin, ginger, and pepper.
6. Cook them until they start boiling. Stir in the tilapia fish pieces and lower the heat. Cook the stew for 12 min.
7. Serve your tilapia stew with couscous.
8. Enjoy.

TURKISH
Poached Eggs with Yogurt Sauce

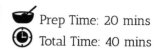 Prep Time: 20 mins

Total Time: 40 mins

Servings per Recipe: 2

Calories	442 kcal
Fat	29.4 g
Carbohydrates	16.2g
Protein	29.1 g
Cholesterol	600 mg
Sodium	1599 mg

Ingredients

3 cloves garlic, peeled and minced

1 1/2 C plain yogurt

1 pinch salt

1 quart water

1 tbsp vinegar

1 tsp salt

6 eggs

2 tbsp butter

1 tsp paprika

Directions

1. Get a small mixing bowl: whisk in it the garlic, yogurt and pinch of salt to make the sauce.
2. Place a large saucepan over high heat. Stir in it the water, vinegar and 1 tsp salt. Cook them until they start boiling.
3. Lower the heat and crack 1 egg at a time into the bubbling water leaving space between them. Let them cook until the white part is done then drain them.
4. Place the eggs on serving plate.
5. Place small pan over medium heat and heat the butter in it. Add to it the paprika and turn off the heat.
6. Drizzle the yogurt sauce over the mix and top it with the paprika butter mix. Serve it warm.
7. Enjoy.

Turkish
Chicken Casserole

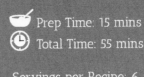

Prep Time: 15 mins
Total Time: 55 mins

Servings per Recipe: 6
Calories	397 kcal
Fat	19.5 g
Carbohydrates	9.4g
Protein	43.7 g
Cholesterol	113 mg
Sodium	854 mg

Ingredients

2 tbsp olive oil, divided

1 1/2 lbs skinless, boneless chicken breast halves - cut into 1 inch cubes

1/2 (12 oz) jar roasted red bell peppers, drained

1 (14.5 oz) can diced tomatoes with juice

1 (6 oz) jar mushrooms, drained

1 onion, diced

1 tbsp minced garlic

Salt and pepper to taste

1 (16 oz) package shredded mozzarella cheese

Directions

1. Before you do anything preheat the oven to 350 f. grease a casserole dish and place it aside.
2. Place a large pan over medium heat and heat 1 tbsp of oil in it. Brown it in the chicken breasts on all sides.
3. Get a food processor: place the jarred peppers in it and process them until they become smooth.
4. Pour it into the casserole dish with the browned chicken, roasted red peppers, tomatoes, mushrooms, onion, and garlic, a pinch of salt and pepper.
5. Stir them well then top them with 1 tbsp of olive oil and mozzarella cheese. Place the casserole in the oven and cook it for 32 min. serve it warm.
6. Enjoy.

WARM
Lentil Salad with Yogurt Sauce

Prep Time: 15 mins
Total Time: 1 hr 40 mins

Servings per Recipe: 4

Calories	352 kcal
Fat	12.3 g
Carbohydrates	46.7g
Protein	15.1 g
Cholesterol	3 mg
Sodium	239 mg

Ingredients

3 tbsp extra-virgin olive oil

1 onion, thinly sliced

1 clove garlic, minced

1 lb carrots cut into thin half-rounds

1 tbsp tomato paste

1/2 tsp ground chile pepper

1/4 tsp sea salt

3 C water

1 C lentil

Salt and freshly ground black pepper to taste

1/4 C Greek yogurt

Directions

1. Place a large pan over medium heat. Add the oil in it and heat it. Sauté in it the onion for 8 min. stirs in the garlic and cook them for 3 min.
2. Add the carrots with tomato paste, ground chile pepper, and sea salt. Cook them for 3 min.
3. Place a large saucepan over medium heat. Stir in it the water with lentils and cook them until they start boiling. Put on the lid and lower the heat then cook it for 32 min.
4. Turn the heat to medium and add the cooked onion mix to the saucepan. Let them cook for 3 min. adjust the seasoning of the mix then serve it warm with some yogurt.
5. Enjoy.

Turkish
Pudding

Prep Time: 10 mins
Total Time: 1 day 2 hrs

Servings per Recipe: 12	
Calories	389 kcal
Fat	3.1 g
Carbohydrates	87.5g
Protein	7.6 g
Cholesterol	0 mg
Sodium	24 mg

Ingredients

For the Pudding:
1/2 C dry garbanzo beans
1/2 C dry white beans
2 C fine bulgur
1/2 C raisins
15 C water
3 C white sugars
1/4 C dried apricots
1/4 C orange peel, chopped
5 whole cloves

For Garnish:
2 tbsp sesame seeds, toasted
2 tbsp chopped walnuts
2 tbsp chopped pistachio nuts
2 tbsp dried currants
1 tbsp ground cinnamon

Directions

1. Place each of the garbanzo beans, white beans, bulgur, and raisins in a bowl of their own then cover them with water. Place them aside to sit for 12 h.
2. Get a large saucepan: stir in the white beans with garbanzo beans and cover them with water. Cook them until they start boiling.
3. Lower the heat and cook them for 1 h to 1 h 30 min while removing the foam that rises on top.
4. Get another large saucepan: place in it the wheat with 15 C of water then cook it until it starts boiling. Lower the heat and cook it for 15 min while removing the foam that rises on top.
5. Add the sugar to the cooking wheat then cook it until it starts boiling again. Remove the beans mix from the water and add it to the saucepan with the wheat and sugar.
6. Add the raisins, apricots, orange peel, and cloves. Lower the heat and cook them for an extra 16 min.
7. Spoon the mix into serving bowl then top them with some nuts like toasted sesame seeds, chopped walnuts, chopped pistachios, currants, and cinnamon.
8. Place the pudding bowls in the fridge to cool down completely then serve it.
9. Enjoy.

RICH
Chicken Pie

Prep Time: 30 mins
Total Time: 1 hr 40 mins

Servings per Recipe: 10

Calories	735 kcal
Fat	28 g
Carbohydrates	86.2g
Protein	31 g
Cholesterol	110 mg
Sodium	685 mg

Directions

1. Mix the flour, 1/2 tsp salt and 1 C water in a mixing bowl until they become smooth. Cut the dough into 2 portions and place them in a greased bowl.
2. Place a wet towel on top and place them aside.
3. Bring a salted pot of water to a boil. Stir in it the 1 tsp salt and a whole peeled onion with chicken. Bring it to a rolling boil until the chicken is done.
4. Drain the chicken discard the bones then place it aside.
5. Before you do anything else preheat the oven to 350 f.
6. Place a large saucepan over medium heat and heat in it 2 tbsp of butter. Stir in the rice and cook it for 3 min.
7. Stir in 1/2 tsp salt and 6 C water then put on the lid and cook them until they start boiling. lower the heat and keep cooking the rice for 12 min.
8. Roll each portion of dough on a floured surface into a round shape that fits in you pie dish.
9. Grease a pie baking dish and place in the bottom of it a round of dough. spoon to it the cooked rice followed by the chicken then lay the second round of dough on top.
10. Cut off the excess dough hanging on the side and brush the pie with a beaten egg. Place the pie in the oven and cook it for 32 min.
11. Once the time is up, serve your pie warm with your favorite toppings.
12. Enjoy..

Ingredients

3 C all-purpose flour
1/2 tsp salt
1 C warm water
1 (2 to 3 lb) whole chicken
Water to cover
1 tsp salt
1 onion, peeled
2 tbsp butter
3 C uncooked white rice
1/2 tsp salt
6 C water
Freshly ground black pepper
1 egg, beaten
1 (10 inch) unbaked pie crust

Creamy
Beef Stew Casserole

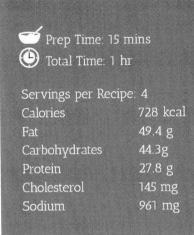

Prep Time: 15 mins
Total Time: 1 hr

Servings per Recipe: 4
Calories	728 kcal
Fat	49.4 g
Carbohydrates	44.3g
Protein	27.8 g
Cholesterol	145 mg
Sodium	961 mg

Ingredients

5 tbsp olive oil

1 lb ground beef

1 tsp ground paprika

1 tsp ground cumin

1 tsp salt

1 tsp ground black pepper

4 potatoes, peeled and cut into 1/2-inch cubes

1 (6.5 oz) can tomato sauce

1 tbsp chopped summer savory (chubritsa)

1 egg, lightly beaten

2/3 C yogurt

Directions

1. Before you do anything preheat the oven to 325 f.
2. Place a large pan over medium heat and heat the oil in it. Add the beef and brown it for 6 to 7 min. stir in the paprika, cumin, salt, and pepper with potato. Cook them for 4 min.
3. Add the tomato sauce, summer savory and some water to cover them. Lower the heat and let them cook for 16 min.
4. Grease a glass baking dish and pour the beef mix into it. Whisk the yogurt with egg in a mixing bowl. Pour the mix all over the beef mix and spread it gently.
5. Place the beef casserole in the oven for 38 min then serve it warm.
6. Enjoy.

SHAKSHOUKA
Breakfast Eggs and Tomato Skillet

🥘 Prep Time: 20 mins
🕐 Total Time: 40 mins

Servings per Recipe: 4
Calories	209 kcal
Fat	15 g
Carbohydrates	12.9g
Protein	7.8 g
Cholesterol	164 mg
Sodium	654 mg

Ingredients

3 tbsp olive oil

1 1/3 C chopped onion

1 C thinly sliced bell peppers, any color

2 cloves garlic, minced, or to taste

2 1/2 C chopped tomatoes

1 tsp ground cumin

1 tsp paprika

1 tsp salt

1 hot chile pepper, seeded and finely chopped, or to taste

4 eggs

Directions

1. Place a large pan over medium heat and heat the oil in it. Sauté in it the onion, bell peppers, and garlic for 6 min.

2. Toss the tomatoes, cumin, paprika, salt, and chile pepper in a large mixing bowl. Add it to the pan and cook them for 12 min over low heat.

3. Use the back of the spoon to make small spaces in the tomato mix for the eggs then crack the eggs in them. Keep the heat on low and cook them for 6 min.

4. Once the time is up, serve you breakfast skillet warm.

5. Enjoy.

Minty
Bulgur Soup

Prep Time: 15 mins
Total Time: 1 hr

Servings per Recipe: 4
Calories	283 kcal
Fat	7.8 g
Carbohydrates	42.7g
Protein	12.2 g
Cholesterol	0 mg
Sodium	94 mg

Ingredients
2 tbsp olive oil, or more to taste
1 onion, finely chopped
Salt to taste
1 tsp ground cayenne pepper
1 tbsp tomato paste
8 C water
3/4 C red lentils
1/4 C white rice

1/4 C fine bulgur
1 clove garlic, minced (optional)
2 tsp crushed dried mint

Directions
1. Place a large pot on medium heat. Add the oil and heat. Stir in it the salt with onion and cook them for 6 min.
2. Lower the heat and stir in the cayenne pepper then cook them for 40 sec.
3. Add the tomato pasta with water and stir them well. Turn the heat up to high then add the lentils, rice, bulgur, garlic, and mint.
4. Cook them until they start boiling then low heat. Put on a partial cover and let them cook for 40 while stirring from time to time. Serve your soup warm.
5. Enjoy..

TURKISH VEGGIE
Lentil Meatballs

Prep Time: 25 mins

Total Time: 45 mins

Servings per Recipe: 7

Calories	208 kcal
Fat	6.8 g
Carbohydrates	29.2g
Protein	9.6 g
Cholesterol	0 mg
Sodium	372 mg

Ingredients

1 3/4 C water

1 C red lentil

3/4 C fine bulgur (cracked wheat)

3 tbsp olive oil

7 spring onions, finely chopped, or more to taste

1 1/2 tbsp tomato paste

1/2 bunch parsley, minced

1/2 lemon, juiced

1 1/2 tsp red pepper flakes

1 tsp ground cumin

1 tsp salt

Directions

1. Stir the lentils with water in a large saucepan. Place it over medium heat and cook it until it starts boiling. Low the heat and cook it for 12 min.

2. Add the bulgur and turn off the heat right away. Put on the lid and let them sit for 6 min.

3. Place a large pan over medium heat. Heat the oil in it. Add the onion and cook it for 4 min. mix in the tomato paste and cook them for another 4 min.

4. Stir in the lentils and bulgur mix then transfer them to a large mixing bowl. Add the parsley, lemon juice, red pepper flakes, cumin, and salt.

5. Mix them with your hands well then shape the mix into small bite size pieces. Serve them with your favorite toppings.

6. Enjoy.

Nutty
Turkish Sweets

Prep Time: 20 mins
Total Time: 3 hrs 30 mins

Servings per Recipe: 12
Calories   302 kcal
Fat   3.5 g
Carbohydrates   66.1g
Protein   3.2 g
Cholesterol   0 mg
Sodium   42 mg

Ingredients

1 1/2 C water

3 C granulated sugars

3 tbsp light corn syrup

1/2 C orange juice

3 tbsp orange zest

3 (.25 oz) envelopes unflavored gelatin

3/4 C cornstarch

1/2 C cold water

1 tbsp vanilla extract

3/4 C chopped pistachio nuts

Confectioners' sugar for dusting

Directions

1. Stir 1 1/2 C water, sugar, and corn syrup in a medium saucepan then place over medium heat. Cook them until they start boiling while stirring all the time until the mix reaches 240 f.
2. Mix in the orange juice, orange zest, and gelatin in a mixing bowl. Place it aside.
3. Stir cornstarch with 1/2 C cold water in a mixing bowl then add it to the hot syrup mix. Turn on the heat to medium low and cook them while stirring gently until the mix thickens.
4. Turn off the heat and add the orange juice mix with pistachios, and vanilla. Sprinkle some confectioner sugar in the bottom of an 8inches baking pan.
5. Pour the syrup mix into it and place it in dark and cold area to lose heat and sit for 3 h 30 min.
6. Top the sweets pan with some confectioner sugar to cover its top then slice it into dices and dust them again with some confectioner sugar then serve them or store them.
7. Enjoy.

TURKISH
Yogurt Bread

Prep Time: 30 mins
Total Time: 4 hrs

Servings per Recipe: 4

Calories	505 kcal
Fat	3.8 g
Carbohydrates	100.2g
Protein	15.1 g
Cholesterol	6 mg
Sodium	1766 mg

Ingredients

1 (.25 oz) package active dry yeast

1 tbsp white sugar

1 tbsp salt

1 1/2 C warm water (110 degrees F/45 degrees C)

1/2 C Greek-style yogurt

4 C all-purpose flour

Directions

1. Stir the warm water with yeast, sugar, and salt in a small bowl.
2. Combine the water mix with yogurt and flour in a large mixing bowl then knead the mix until you get soft dough.
3. Sprinkle some flour on a working surface and shape the dough on it into a ball. Place a wet towel on it and let it rest for 3 h 10 min.
4. Shape the dough into 4 pieces and flatten each one of them in a round shape. Place them on lined up baking sheet and cover them with a wet towel then let them rise for 16 min.
5. Place a large griddle pan over medium heat and heat it. Place a piece of round dough in the griddle and cook it for 1 to 2 min on each side or until is done.
6. Repeat the process with the rest of the dough loaves. Serve your bread loaves warm.
7. Enjoy.

Garlicky
Cream Dip

Prep Time: 20 mins
Total Time: 8 hrs 30 mins

Servings per Recipe: 8
Calories	92 kcal
Fat	5.9 g
Carbohydrates	5.7g
Protein	4.5 g
Cholesterol	19 mg
Sodium	88 mg

Ingredients

1 (16 oz) container plain yogurt
5 cloves garlic
1 pinch salt
1 bunch fresh dill, chopped
1 bunch fresh parsley, chopped
1 (4 oz) package cream cheese, softened

(optional)
2 mint leaves, for garnish

Directions

1. Get a mixing bowl: place a colander or sieve on top of it then cover it with piece of cheesecloth making two layers of them.
2. Pour the yogurt into the colander and cover it with a piece of plastic. Let it sit for 9 h.
3. Once the time is up, pour the strained yogurt into a medium mixing bowl.
4. Combine the salt with garlic in a mortar and press them until you get a smooth paste. Add it to the strained yogurt with the dill, parsley, and cream cheese.
5. Scoop the yogurt dip into a serving plate or bowl then serve it with a swirl of olive oil.
6. Enjoy.

WEDDING
Lentils Soup

Prep Time: 10 mins
Total Time: 1 hr 25 mins

Servings per Recipe: 4
Calories	442 kcal
Fat	14 g
Carbohydrates	64.2g
Protein	18.7 g
Cholesterol	31 mg
Sodium	1080 mg

Ingredients
1/4 C butter
2 onions, finely chopped
1 tsp paprika
1 C red lentil
1/2 C fine bulgur
2 tbsp tomato paste
8 C vegetable stocks
1/8 tsp cayenne pepper

1 tbsp dried mint leaves
4 slices lemon
1/2 tsp chopped fresh mint

Directions
1. Place a large a large pot over low heat. Heat the butter in it. Add the onion and cook it for 16 min.
2. Add the paprika, lentils, and bulgur, tomato paste, vegetable stock, and cayenne pepper. Cook them until they start boiling. Lower the heat and put on the lid.
3. Keep cooking the soup for 1 h. crush the mint leaves and add them to the soup with then turn off the heat. Serve your soup warm.
4. Enjoy.

Turkish
Chicken Stew II

🥣 Prep Time: 20 mins
🕐 Total Time: 8 hrs 30 mins

Servings per Recipe: 8
Calories	92 kcal
Fat	5.9 g
Carbohydrates	5.7g
Protein	4.5 g
Cholesterol	19 mg
Sodium	88 mg

Ingredients

1 (4 lb) chicken, cut into pieces

1 medium whole potato, peeled

1 small whole onion, peeled

1 small whole carrot, peeled

4 C water

1 1/2 tsp salt

2 (1 inch thick) slices stale French bread, crusts removed

14 oz walnuts, ground

2 cloves garlic, crushed

2 tsp ground red pepper

1 tsp salt

Directions

1. Place a pot over medium heat. Stir in it the chicken, potato, onion and carrot then cover them with the water. Cook them until they start boiling while removing the foam that rises on top.
2. Add 1 1/2 tsp salt then lower the heat and cook them for 1 h with the lid on. Once the time is up, drain the chicken and veggies mix then place the broth aside for later use.
3. Allow the chicken to lose heat slightly then remove the bones with skin and discard them. Cut the chicken into small bite size pieces.
4. Place the bread slices in a mixing bowl and cover them with some of the reserved both. Let them sit for 3 to 5 min then squeeze them dry.
5. Transfer the squeezed bread to a large mixing bowl with the ground walnuts, garlic, red pepper, and 1 tsp salt then combine them well.
6. Spoon the mix into a piece of cheesecloth and tie it then press it with your hands to remove the walnut oil from it into a large bowl.
7. Transfer the squeezed walnut mix to a large mixing bowl then adds to it 1 C of the reserved broth gradually while whisking all the time.
8. Toss the chicken pieces with 3 tbsp of the walnuts mix then place it on a serving deep dish.
9. Pour the rest of the walnuts mix on top to cover the chicken then drizzle the walnut oil on top.
10. Serve it warm with your favorite toppings and some flat bread.

EGGPLANT
Boats

Prep Time: 30 mins
Total Time: 1 hr 25 mins

Servings per Recipe: 2
Calories	314 kcal
Fat	20.8 g
Carbohydrates	28.7g
Protein	5.3 g
Cholesterol	0 mg
Sodium	391 mg

Ingredients

1 eggplant
1 (14.5 oz) can diced tomatoes, drained
1 tbsp tomato paste
1 medium onion, chopped
1 tbsp minced garlic, or to taste
1 tsp ground cinnamon, or to taste

3 tbsp olive oil
Salt and pepper to taste

Directions

1. Before you do anything preheat the oven to 350 f.
2. Cut each eggplant into half lengthwise then scoop out the flesh from the middle gently leaving the eggplant shell intact.
3. Finely chop the eggplant flesh and place it aside.
4. place the eggplant shell boats on a lined up baking sheet and drizzle some olive oil on them then cook them in the oven for 32 min.
5. Place a large pan over medium heat. Heat 2 tbsp of olive oil in it. Sauté in it the garlic with onion for 3 min. stirs in the eggplant flesh and cook them for another 3 min.
6. Add the tomato paste with tomato then low heat and let them cook until the eggplant shells in the oven are done.
7. Once the time is up, get the eggplant shell boats from the oven and place them aside to lose heat slightly. Spoon the tomato mix into them.
8. Place the stuffed eggplant shell boats in the oven and cook them for 32 min then serve them warm.
9. Enjoy..

Flaming Hot
Turkish Ceviche

🥣 Prep Time: 20 mins

🕐 Total Time: 1 hrs 30 mins

Servings per Recipe: 8

Calories	207 kcal
Fat	13 g
Carbohydrates	9.9g
Protein	16.2 g
Cholesterol	129 mg
Sodium	882 mg

Ingredients

1 lemon, halved and seeded

1 head garlic, halved

3 Turkish bay leaves

8 whole black peppercorns

1 tbsp kosher salt, or to taste

1 1/2 lbs peeled and deveined large shrimp (21 to 25 per lb)

2 C coconut milk

1/2 C lime juice

2 Serrano Chile peppers, thinly sliced

1/2 bunch cilantro, chopped

1 red onion, thinly sliced

8 sprigs cilantro, for garnish

1 lime, cut into 8 wedges

Directions

1. Press the lemon halves to squeeze the juice from them into a large pot then add them it as well with the garlic, bay leaves, peppercorns, and salt.
2. Add enough water to fill half of the pot then cook over high heat until it starts boiling.
3. Add the shrimp to the mix and turn off the heat. let them sit for 6 min. remove the shrimp the water mix and place it in a colander the dry it.
4. Spread the shrimp on a lined up baking sheet and place it in the fridge for 32 min.
5. Once the time is up, stir the coconut milk, lime juice, serrano peppers, chopped cilantro, and onion in a mixing bowl with a pinch of salt.
6. Slice the shrimp in half lengthwise then stir it into the mix. Put on the lid and lid and place it in the fridge for 32 min. once the time is up, serve your shrimp Ceviche.
7. Enjoy.

BULGUR
Salad

🥣 Prep Time: 15 mins

🕐 Total Time: 1 hr

Servings per Recipe: 6

Calories	323 kcal
Fat	8.1 g
Carbohydrates	53.1g
Protein	12.8 g
Cholesterol	0 mg
Sodium	511 mg

Ingredients

3 tbsp olive oil

1 onion, minced

1 ripe tomato, cut into small cubes

3 C beef broth

2 C bulgur, rinsed

Salt and ground black pepper, or to taste

1/2 C cooked green lentils

1/3 C cooked chickpeas

1 bunch fresh mint, chopped

Directions

1. Place a large pan over medium heat. Heat the oil in it the sauté in it the onion for 4 min. add the tomato and cook them for 3 min.

2. Stir in the beef broth then cook them until they start boiling. Add the bulgur with a pinch of salt and pepper. Lower the heat and let them cook for 6 min.

3. Stir in the lentils with the chickpeas and cook them for an extra 6 min.

4. Place the mix aside to lose heat for 35 min. once the time is up, stir the mint into it then serve it with your favorite toppings.

5. Enjoy..

Bulgur
Salad II

Prep Time: 20 mins
Total Time: 40 mins

Servings per Recipe: 6
Calories   216 kcal
Fat   9.8 g
Carbohydrates   30.4g
Protein   5.3 g
Cholesterol   0 mg
Sodium   19 mg

Ingredients

1 C fine bulgur

1 C boiling water

2 tbsp olive oil

1 onion, finely chopped

2 large tomatoes, finely chopped

1 cucumber, diced

2 green bell peppers, finely chopped

1 red bell pepper, finely chopped

7 green onions, finely chopped

1/2 C minced fresh parsley

1/2 C minced fresh mint leaves

1 tsp red pepper flakes, or to taste

2 tbsp olive oil

Juice of 1 fresh lemon

2 tbsp pomegranate molasses

Directions

1. Get a large bowl: combine in it the bulgur with the boiling water. Put on the lid and let sit for 22 min.
2. Place a large pan over medium heat and heat 2 tbsp of olive oil in it. Sauté in it the onion for 6 min.
3. Pour the bulgur into a piece of cheesecloth and press it to remove the excess water.
4. Combine it in another large mixing bowl with the onion, chopped tomatoes, cucumber, green and red bell peppers, green onions, parsley, mint, and red pepper flakes, 2 tbsp olive oil, the lemon juice, and the pomegranate molasses.
5. Stir them well and adjust their seasoning then serve it.
6. Enjoy.

AUTHENTIC
Baklava

Prep Time: 30 mins

Total Time: 1 hr 30 mins

Servings per Recipe: 24

Calories	434 kcal
Fat	27 g
Carbohydrates	45.1g
Protein	7.5 g
Cholesterol	31 mg
Sodium	93 mg

Directions

1. Before you do anything preheat the oven to 350 f.
2. Place a large saucepan over medium heat. Stir in 2 C sugar, water, honey, cinnamon stick, lemon and vanilla. Cook them until they start boiling.
3. Lower the heat and let them cook for 16 min while discarding any foam that rise on top to make the syrup.
4. Mix the chopped almonds, 2 tbsp sugar, ground cinnamon and cloves in a small mixing bowl. Place it aside.
5. Grease a 9 inches baking dish with some butter. Cut each phyllo sheet into half. Place a phyllo sheet in the bottom of the dish then coated with melted butter on top.
6. Do the same thing with another 7 phyllo sheets to make a layer with 8 sheets in total. Top it with 1/4 C of almonds mix.
7. Cover the nuts layer with 4 phyllo sheets while brushing each one with melted butter after placing it then top them with 1/4 to 1/3 C of the almonds mix.
8. Repeat the process to make more layers until you are left with 8 sheets.
9. Place the 8 sheets on top the same as the other while brushing them with butter then tuck their edges down. Drizzle the rest of the melted butter on top.
10. Use a sharp knife to make 5 slashes in the phyllo layers diagonally then cut the same way from the other side to make them look like diamonds.
11. Place the pan in the oven and cook it for 1 h until it becomes golden brown. Pour the hot syrup on top of the hot baklava right away then go over the diamond shapes with a knife to cut.
12. Place the baklava pan aside to lose heat then serve it with some ice cream.
13. Enjoy.

Ingredients

2 C white sugars
2 C water
1 C honey
1 cinnamon stick
1/4 lemon
1 tsp vanilla extract
1 1/2 lbs chopped almonds
2 tbsp white sugar
1 tsp ground cinnamon
1/2 tsp ground cloves
1 1/2 C unsalted butter, melted
1 (16 oz) package frozen phyllo pastry, thawed

Authentic Baklava

40

Chicken Tava
Roasted Pepperoncini
Chicken Pan

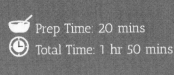

Prep Time: 20 mins
Total Time: 1 hr 50 mins

Servings per Recipe: 8
Calories	316 kcal
Fat	13.7 g
Carbohydrates	29 g
Protein	20.4 g
Cholesterol	59 mg
Sodium	823 mg

Ingredients

2 tbsp olive oil, divided

8 boneless chicken thighs, with skin

1 (6 oz) can tomato paste

1/4 C water

8 cloves garlic, halved

Salt and pepper to taste

4 medium potatoes, sliced

4 tomatoes, sliced

1 large onion, sliced

1 C fresh mushrooms, sliced

8 Pepperoncini peppers

Directions

1. Before you do anything preheat the oven to 325 f.
2. Whisk the tomato paste water in a small bowl.
3. Brush a roasting pan with 1 tbsp of olive oil. Lay in it the chicken thighs. Pour the tomato paste mix all over it then top it with garlic halves, a pinch of salt and pepper.
4. Surround it with the veggies then drizzle the rest of the oil on top. Roast the chicken veggies pan in the oven for 1 h 32 min then serve it warm.
5. Enjoy.

HOW TO MAKE
Turkish Kebabs

🍲 Prep Time: 15 mins
🕐 Total Time: 30 mins

Servings per Recipe: 6
Calories	667 kcal
Fat	36.2 g
Carbohydrates	48.6g
Protein	37.3 g
Cholesterol	144 mg
Sodium	886 mg

Ingredients

4 pita bread rounds

1 tbsp olive oil

4 skinless, boneless chicken breast
halves - chopped

2 medium onion, chopped

1 clove garlic, minced

1 (10.75 oz) can tomato puree

Ground cumin to taste

Salt to taste

Ground black pepper to taste

1/2 C butter, melted

1 C Greek yogurt

1/4 C chopped fresh parsley

Directions

1. Before you do anything preheat the oven to 350 f.

2. Lay the pita bread round on a lined p baking pan. Cook them in the oven for 3 min. slice them into small pieces and place them aside.

3. Place a large pan over medium heat. Heat the oil in it. Add the onion with garlic and chicken then cook them for 6 min.

4. Add the tomato purée with cumin, a pinch of salt and pepper. Le they cook for 12 min.

5. Once the time is up, lay the pita pieces on a serving plate then top them with the melted butter, chicken and yogurt. Serve it right away.

6. Enjoy. .

Muhammara
Aleppo Walnuts Dip

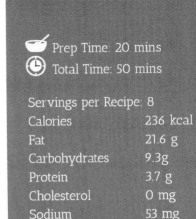

Prep Time: 20 mins
Total Time: 50 mins

Servings per Recipe: 8
Calories   236 kcal
Fat   21.6 g
Carbohydrates   9.3g
Protein   3.7 g
Cholesterol   0 mg
Sodium   53 mg

Ingredients

2 sweet bell peppers, seeded and quartered
3 slices whole wheat bread, crusts removed
3/4 C toasted walnuts, chopped
2 tbsp lemon juice
2 tbsp Aleppo pepper

2 tsp pomegranate molasses
1 clove garlic, minced
1 tsp cumin seeds, coarsely ground
Salt to taste
1/2 C olive oil
1 pinch sumac powder

Directions

1. Before you do anything preheat the oven broiler. Place the rack 6 inches away from the heat.
2. Lay the bell peppers on a foil lined up baking sheet with the cut up sides facing down. Cook them in the oven for 7 min until they are well roasted.
3. Place the bread in a toaster and toast them. Place the bread slices aside to lose heat completely then process them in a food processor until they become crumbled.
4. Wrap the peppers in a piece of plastic bag and let them lose heat and soften for a while. Discard the skin of the peppers and clean them well.
5. Place them in a mixing bowl and use a fork to mash them.
6. Get a food processor: combine in it the mashed roasted peppers with bread crumbs, walnuts, lemon juice, Aleppo pepper, pomegranate molasses, garlic, cumin, and salt.
7. Process them several times until they are well combined. Add the olive oil gradually while processing all the time until you use all the oil and get a smooth mix.
8. Pour the dip into a serving bowl and top it with a pinch of sumac then serve it.
9. Enjoy.

DOLMAS
Stuffed Grape Leaves

🥣 Prep Time: 30 mins
🕐 Total Time: 1 h 30 mins

Servings per Recipe: 8
Calories	207 kcal
Fat	3.8 g
Carbohydrates	39.1g
Protein	5.3 g
Cholesterol	0 mg
Sodium	847 mg

Ingredients

1 tbsp olive oil

2 onions, minced

1 1/2 C uncooked white rice

2 tbsp tomato paste

2 tbsp dried currants

2 tbsp pine nuts

1 tbsp ground cinnamon

1 tbsp dried mint

1 tbsp dried dill weed

1 tsp ground allspice

1 tsp ground cumin

1 (8 oz) jar grape leaves, drained and rinsed

Directions

1. Place a saucepan over medium heat. Heat the oil in it. Add the onion and cook it for 3 min. combine in the rice then cover them with hot water.

2. Put on the lid and cook them over low medium heat for 12 min. turn off the heat then add the tomato paste, currants, pine nuts, cinnamon, mint leaves, dill weed, allspice and cumin.

3. Stir them well then place the mix aside to lose heat. Run the grape leaves under some cool water then drain them and discard their stems.

4. Lay a grape leaf on a working surface and place in the center of it 1 tsp of the nutty rice mix.

5. Roll the sides of the leaf to the middle then roll it to the front to keep the stuffing inside. Repeat the process with the rest of the ingredients.

6. Place a large pan over medium low heat then lay in it the stuffed grapes leaves in the pot and cover them warm water. Put on the lid and cook them for 40 min while adding more water if needed.

7. Once the time is up, drain your grape finger then serve them.

8. Enjoy..

Rosy Turkish
Borscht

Prep Time: 20 mins
Total Time: 1 hr 5 mins

Servings per Recipe: 8
Calories   128 kcal
Fat   5 g
Carbohydrates   19.8g
Protein   3 g
Cholesterol   11 mg
Sodium   908 mg

Ingredients

1 1/2 C thinly sliced potatoes

1 C thinly sliced beets

4 C vegetable stock or water

2 tbsp butter

1 1/2 C chopped onions

1 tsp caraway seed (optional)

2 tsp salt

1 celery stalk, chopped

1 large carrot, sliced

3 C coarsely chopped red cabbage

Black pepper to taste

1/4 tsp fresh dill weed

1 tbsp cider vinegar

1 tbsp honey

1 C tomato puree

Sour cream, for topping

Chopped tomatoes, for garnish

Directions

1. Place a large saucepan over medium heat. Stir in it the potato slices with beets and stock. Cook them until they start boiling. Lower the heat and cook them until they soften.
2. Drain the cooked veggies and place the stock aside.
3. Place a large pan over medium heat and heat the butter in it. Add the onions, caraway seeds, and salt then sauté them for 3 min.
4. Add the celery, carrots, and cabbage with the stock. Put on the lid and let them for 12 min until the veggies become soft.
5. Stir in the cooked potato with beets, a pinch of salt and pepper, cider vinegar, honey, and tomato puree. Put on the lid and lower the heat. Cook them for 32 min.
6. Once the time is up, serve your borscht warm as it is with some yogurt or purée it.
7. Enjoy.

PERSIAN
Orange and Bean Stew

Prep Time: 12 mins
Total Time: 1 h

Servings per Recipe: 4
Calories   493.2
Fat   6.5g
Cholesterol   0.0mg
Sodium   2222.4mg
Carbohydrates   85.6g
Protein   26.1g

Ingredients

1 tbsp olive oil

2 onions, chopped

3 cloves garlic, chopped

1 tsp salt

1 tsp cumin

1/4 tsp cinnamon

1 C. orange juice

1 lime, juice of

1 can tomato paste

4 (15 1/2 oz.) cans kidney beans, rinsed and drained

1 jalapeno, chopped

pita bread

Directions

1. Place a large skillet over medium heat. Heat the oil in it. Add the onion and cook it for 6 min.
2. Stir in the spices and cook them for another 6 min. Add the orange and lime juice. Cook them until they start boiling. Cook them for 12 min over low heat.
3. Stir in the peppers with beans. Cook them for 22 min. cook them for 5 min. serve your stew warm.
4. Enjoy...

Persian
Potato Rice Stew

🥣 Prep Time: 3 hrs
🕐 Total Time: 3 hr 45 mins

Servings per Recipe: 6
Calories   499.7
Fat   9.7g
Cholesterol   0.0mg
Sodium   11.4mg
Carbohydrates   92.5g
Protein   8.7g

Ingredients

3 C. of white long grain rice
4 tbsp cooking oil
3 - 4 medium potatoes
4 oz. water
salt

Directions

1. Get a large bowl: Place in it the rice and cover it with hot water and a pinch of salt. Place it aside.
2. Remove the peel of the potato and slice them.
3. Place a medium pot and fill half of it with water. Place in it the rice and cook it until it starts boiling. Once the rice is half done drain it.
4. Place a large pot over medium heat. Heat the oil in it. Stir in the water. Spread the potato in the pot and sprinkle on it some sat. Top it with rice.
5. Make a hole in the center of the rice layer and another 4 holes on the side. Drizzle some water on top. Put on the lid and cook them for 3 min over high heat.
6. Lower the heat and drizzle some oil top. Lower the heat to medium heat and cook it for 16 min.
7. Lower the heat to medium low. Drizzle more of some oil on top then cook it for 12 min. serve your potato rice warm.
8. Enjoy.

PERSIAN
Basmati Rice

🥣 Prep Time: 10 mins
🕐 Total Time: 35 mins

Servings per Recipe: 4
Calories	280.1
Fat	9.7g
Cholesterol	15.2mg
Sodium	373.5mg
Carbohydrates	44.2g
Protein	5.2g

Ingredients

2 tbsp butter
1 C. white basmati rice, rinsed under cold
water in a fine mesh sieve
1/2 tsp salt
1/4 tsp cracked black pepper
1 garlic clove, minced
orange peel
1/2 tsp ground cinnamon

1/4 tsp curry powder
2 C. water
3 tbsp roasted pistachios
3 tbsp golden raisins

Directions

1. Place a large skillet over medium heat. Stir in it the rice for 5 min while stirring it.
2. Add the salt, pepper, garlic, orange peel, cinnamon and curry powder. Cook them for 2 min. Stir in the water and put on the lid. Lower the heat.
3. Cook them for 26 min. Place the cover aside and add to it the pistachios and golden raisins. Discard the orange peel. Serve your nutty rice warm.
4. Enjoy.

Persian
Pistachios and Bean Pilaf

🥣 Prep Time: 20 mins
🕐 Total Time: 50 mins

Servings per Recipe: 4
Calories   411.0
Fat   15.6g
Cholesterol   0.0mg
Sodium   215.8mg
Carbohydrates   56.2g
Protein   15.4g

Ingredients

150 g frozen broad beans

1 tbsp olive oil

1 large kumara, peeled, cut into 2cm cubes (orange sweet potato)

1 brown onion, finely chopped

2 tsp finely grated ginger

1 tsp ground cumin

1 tsp ground coriander

1 tsp ground turmeric

1 tsp ground paprika

190 g quinoa, rinsed, drained

500 ml vegetable stock

1 bunch kale, stems trimmed, shredded

75 g pistachios, toasted, coarsely chopped

1/2 C. coriander leaves

lemon wedge, to serve

Directions

1. Before you do anything preheat the oven to 400 F. Cover a baking sheet with a piece of parchment paper.
2. Lay the kumara in the baking sheet and drizzle some of the oil on it. Sprinkle some salt and pepper on it. Cook it in the oven for 22 min.
3. Bring a large saucepan of water to a boil. Add the broad beans and cook it 3 min. Drain it and rinse it with cool water. Remove the broad bean peel.
4. Place a large saucepan over medium heat. Heat the rest of the oil in it. Sauté in it the onion for 6 min.
5. Stir in the ginger, cumin, coriander, turmeric and paprika. Sauté them for 2 min.
6. Combine the stock with quinoa in a large saucepan. Cook them until they start boiling. Lower the heat and put on the lid. Cook them for 16 min.
7. Add the kale and cook them for 2 min. Stir in the kumara, broad beans and pistachios, salt and pepper. Serve your Pilaf warm.
8. Enjoy.

PERSIAN
Noodles Bean Soup

🥣 Prep Time: 2 hrs
🕐 Total Time: 3 hrs 45 mins

Servings per Recipe: 8	
Calories	414.9
Fat	23.5g
Cholesterol	2.7mg
Sodium	563.9mg
Carbohydrates	43.8g
Protein	11.7g

Ingredients

100 g chickpeas
100 g lentils
100 g navy beans or 100 g kidney beans
250 g flat wheat noodles
1/2 C. coriander, chopped
1/2 C. spinach, chopped
1/2 C. chives, chopped
1/2 C. dill, chopped
1/2 C. parsley, chopped
1/2 C. oil
3 tbsp plain flour

1 C. buttermilk
2 tbsp sour cream
1/2 tsp turmeric
1/2 tsp ground black pepper, to taste
100 g walnuts (kernels)
1/4 C. crushed dried mint
1/2 tbsp salt, to taste
4 medium onions
6 C. water
9 C. water
1/2 C. water

Directions

1. Soak the chickpeas in some water for 2 h 30 min. Place a large pot over medium heat. Pour 6 C. of water in the pot. Add the chickpeas and cook it for 45 min.
2. Clean the lentils with some water. Stir them into the pot and cook them for 25 min while stirring often. Clean it.
3. Clean the herbs with some water and dry them.
4. Place a large pan over medium heat. Heat 1/4 C. oil in it. Chop the onion and cook in it for 6 min. Place half of it aside. Stir in the turmeric and cook them for 2 min.
5. Stir the cooked turmeric onion with 9 C. of water and noodles. Cook them for 6 min.
6. Whisk half C. of water with flour until they become smooth. Stir it with the chopped herbs into the pot. Lower the heat and cook them for 42 min.
7. Add the buttermilk with sour cream. Cook them for 3 min.
8. Heat 1/4 C. of oil in it in a large pan. Cook in it the dry mint for 2 min. Serve your soup hot with the dried mint warm.
9. Enjoy.

Persian
Lemon Chicken Kabobs

Prep Time: 10 mins
Total Time: 50 mins

Servings per Recipe: 4
Calories	432.4
Fat	33.7g
Cholesterol	92.8mg
Sodium	673.4mg
Carbohydrates	1.1g
Protein	30.3g

Ingredients

4 boneless chicken breasts, cut in cubes

6 tbsp olive oil

1/16 tsp saffron, crushed

3 tbsp lemon juice

1 tsp salt

1/4 tsp pepper

1/4 tsp basil

1/4 tsp turmeric

1/4 tsp garlic powder

Directions

1. Get a large mixing bowl: Stir into it all the ingredients. Place it in the fridge for 2 h 30 min.
2. Preheat the grill and grease its grates.
3. Thread the chicken pieces into skewers and cook them on the grill for 35 min while turning them often. Serve your kabobs warm.
4. Enjoy.

PERSIAN
Chicken Wings Soup

🍲 Prep Time: 20 mins

🕐 Total Time: 1 hr 30 mins

Servings per Recipe: 8

Calories	656.2
Fat	36.0g
Cholesterol	165.3mg
Sodium	934.2mg
Carbohydrates	34.0g
Protein	47.9g

Ingredients

1/4 C. canola oil
1 lb chicken wings
kosher salt & freshly ground black pepper, to taste
3 medium onions (2 roughly chopped, 1 minced)
3 medium carrots, roughly chopped
2 garlic cloves, crushed
8 C. chicken stock

1 bay leaf
1 1/2 lbs ground chicken
1 1/2 C. chickpea flour
2 1/2 tsp ground turmeric
2 tsp ground coriander
1 1/2 tsp baking soda
1/2 tsp ground cardamom

Directions

1. Place a soup pot over medium heat. Heat 3 tbsp of oil in it.
2. Sprinkle some salt and pepper over the chicken wings. Brown it in the pot for 14 min. Stir in the onions, carrots, and garlic. Sauté them for 10 min.
3. Stir in the stock, bay leaf, and salt. Cook them until they start boiling. Lower the heat and cook the soup for 37 min.
4. Pour the broth in a colander and drain it. Discard the chicken wings with veggies. Pour the broth into the pot.
5. Heat the oil in a large pan. Add the onion and cook them for 5 min. Allow it to cool down slightly.
6. Get a large mixing bowl: Combine in it the rest of the ingredients and mix them well. Shape the mix into meatballs.
7. Stir the meatballs into the hot broth. Cook them until they start simmering. Put on half a cover over the pot. Cook the soup for 18 min. Serve your soup warm.
8. Enjoy.

Potato and Pepper
Meatballs

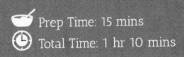 Prep Time: 15 mins

🕐 Total Time: 1 hr 10 mins

Servings per Recipe: 6
Calories	188.5
Fat	3.3g
Cholesterol	124.0mg
Sodium	88.8mg
Carbohydrates	32.2g
Protein	7.9g

Ingredients

5 medium potatoes or 600 g potatoes

4 eggs

1 medium green bell pepper, chopped

1/4 tsp saffron

salt

pepper

1/2 tsp baking powder

frying oil

Directions

1. Bring a salted pot of water to a boil. Cook in it the potato until it becomes soft. Drain it and place it aside.
2. Place the potato in a grater and grate it.
3. Get a large mixing bowl: Mix in it the potato with eggs, bell pepper, a pinch of salt and pepper. Mix them well. Add the saffron with baking powder. Mix them again.
4. Place a large skillet over medium heat. Heat the oil in it. Shape the mix into patties and cook them in the pan for 10 min on each side with the lid on.
5. Serve your potato patties warm.
6. Enjoy..

PERSIAN
Chicken Berries Pilaf

Prep Time: 15 mins
Total Time: 1 hr 10 mins

Servings per Recipe: 4
Calories	1371.1
Fat	77.8g
Cholesterol	279.9mg
Sodium	567.0mg
Carbohydrates	129.0g
Protein	43.7g

Ingredients

7 oz. raisins

6 oz. barberries

6 onions, large

1/2 lb butter

salt, to taste

pepper, to taste

8 chicken thighs

2 C. basmati rice

Directions

1. Before you do anything preheat the oven to 400 F.
2. Place a large pan over medium heat. Heat 2 oz. of butter until it melts. Sprinkle some salt and pepper over the chicken thighs. Coat it with some of the melted butter.
3. Lay the chicken thighs on a lined up baking sheet. Cook it in the oven for 48 min.
4. Cut the onion into slices. Cook it in the pan with a pinch of salt for 4 min. Add the raisins with barberries. Cook them for 1 min. Turn off the heat and let the mix cool down slightly.
5. Put the chicken thighs on a serving plate and top them with rice and onion berries mix. Serve it warm.
6. Enjoy.

Persian Lime Lamb Stew

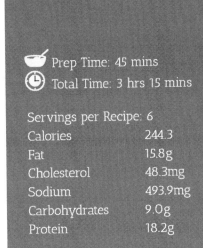

🥣 Prep Time: 45 mins
🕐 Total Time: 3 hrs 15 mins

Servings per Recipe: 6	
Calories	244.3
Fat	15.8g
Cholesterol	48.3mg
Sodium	493.9mg
Carbohydrates	9.0g
Protein	18.2g

Ingredients

2 large onions, peeled and thinly sliced

1 lb stew meat, cut in 1-inch cubes (lamb, veal or beef)

1/3 C. oil

1 tsp salt

1/2 tsp ground black pepper

1/2 tsp turmeric

5 stalks celery, washed and cut into 1 inch lengths

3 C. chopped fresh parsley

1/2 chopped of fresh mint

1/3 C. fresh squeezed lime juice

Directions

1. Place a pot over medium heat. Add 3 tbsp of oil and heat it. Cook in it the lamb meat with onion, turmeric, a pinch of salt and pepper. Cook them for 4 min.
2. Stir in 2 C. of water. Put on the lid and cook them for 35 min.
3. Place a large pan over medium heat. Heat 3 tbsp of oil in it. Add the celery and sauté it for 12 min. Stir in the herbs and cook them for 12 min.
4. Transfer the mix to the pot with lime juice. Put on the lid and cook them for 1 h 35 min. Adjust the seasoning of the soup then serve it warm.
5. Enjoy.

PERSIAN
Zucchini Omelet

Prep Time: 10 mins
Total Time: 1 hr

Servings per Recipe: 6

Calories	80.1
Fat	3.5g
Cholesterol	141.0mg
Sodium	160.6mg
Carbohydrates	7.2g
Protein	5.5g

Ingredients

2 medium onions, chopped
4 garlic cloves, minced
1 lb zucchini, grated
4 eggs
1/2 tsp turmeric
1/2 tsp baking soda

salt and pepper
olive oil
cooking spray

Directions

1. Place a large pan over medium heat. Heat the oil in it. Sauté in it the turmeric with onion for 3 min.
2. Add the zucchini with a pinch of salt and pepper. Cook them for 4 min.
3. Get a large mixing bowl: Beat the eggs in it. Add the baking soda with a pinch of salt and pepper. Whisk them again. Fold in the onion and zucchini mix.
4. Before you do anything preheat the oven to 375 F.
5. Pour the mix into a greased baking dish. Cook it in the oven for 35 min. Serve it warm.
6. Enjoy.

Persian
Spinach Omelet

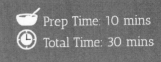 Prep Time: 10 mins

 Total Time: 30 mins

Servings per Recipe: 3
Calories   328.1
Fat   20.2g
Cholesterol   423.0mg
Sodium   769.3mg
Carbohydrates   19.2g
Protein   21.9g

Ingredients

2 lbs fresh baby spinach leaves

1/4 C. water

2 tbsp oil

2 medium onions, sliced thin (1 C.)

1/2 tsp salt (to taste)

1/8 tsp ground turmeric

1/8 tsp pepper

6 eggs

Directions

1. Pour 1/4 C. of water in a medium sauce. Pour into it 1/4 C. of water in it. Put on the lid and cook them for 6 min. Turn off the heat and let the spinach sit for 6 min.
2. Drain the spinach and squeeze it from the water.
3. Place a large pan over medium heat. Heat the oil in it. Add the onion with turmeric, a pinch of salt and pepper. Cook them for 4 min.
4. Stir in the spinach for 4 min. Make 6 holes in them. Crack an egg in each hole. Cook them for 6 min over low heat until the eggs are done. Serve your skillet warm.
5. Enjoy.

POMEGRANATE
Lamb with Fruit Salad

🥣 Prep Time: 30 mins
🕐 Total Time: 4 hrs

Servings per Recipe: 6
Calories	95.5
Fat	4.8g
Cholesterol	0.0mg
Sodium	10.6mg
Carbohydrates	14.4g
Protein	1.4g

Ingredients

4 tbsp pomegranate molasses

1 tsp ground cumin

1 lemon, juice of

1 tbsp olive oil

2 garlic cloves, minced

1 onion, roughly chopped

1 lamb shoulder, weighing about 1 . 6kg, lightly scored

2 pomegranates, seeds only

handful flat leaf parsley

100 g watercress

1 small red onion, finely diced

1 tbsp olive oil

flat bread, to serve

Directions

1. Before you do anything preheat the oven to 320 F.
2. Get a small mixing bowl: Stir in it the molasses with the cumin, lemon juice, olive oil and garlic to make the sauce.
3. Spread the onion in a greased casserole dish. Place the lamb on it and pour the sauce all over it. Pour 3/4 over the lamb mix.
4. Place a large piece of foil over the casserole dish. Cook it in the oven for 3 h 30 min.
5. Toss the red onion with pomegranate and olive oil in a large salad bowl. Serve it with the roasted lamb warm.
6. Enjoy.

Persian Creamy Dill Chicken Salad

🥣 Prep Time: 10 mins
🕐 Total Time: 1 hr 20 mins

Servings per Recipe: 6

Calories	268.4
Fat	8.4g
Cholesterol	124.7mg
Sodium	842.5mg
Carbohydrates	35.4g
Protein	13.0g

Ingredients

5 white potatoes
3 dill pickles
1 onion, halved
1 1/2 C. green peas, frozen
3 carrots, peeled
1 chicken breast

3 eggs
4 tbsp white vinegar
4 tbsp light mayonnaise
1/2 tsp turmeric
salt and pepper

Directions

1. Pour 2 C. of water in a pot and cook it until it starts boiling. Add the chicken breast, onion, carrots, turmeric, and some salt. Cook them for 50 min. Allow the mix to cool down.
2. Drain the onion and discard it. Drain the chicken and shred it. Place it aside. Dice the carrots and place them aside.
3. Combine the potato with eggs in another pot and cover them with water. Cook them for 14 min. Peel the eggs and place them aside. Peel the potatoes and dice them. Dice the pickles.
4. Get a large mixing bowl: Toss in it the potatoes, chicken, carrots, pickles, peas, and eggs.
5. Get a small mixing bowl: Mix in it the vinegar with mayonnaise, a pinch of salt and pepper. Add the mix to the veggies and chicken. Serve your salad.
6. Enjoy..

PERSIAN
Lentil and Meatball Soup

Prep Time: 20 mins
Total Time: 1 hr 20 mins

Servings per Recipe: 6
Calories   145.6
Fat   6.1g
Cholesterol   31.0mg
Sodium   811.2mg
Carbohydrates   11.9g
Protein   10.6g

Ingredients

Soup:
1/4 C. lentils
1/4 C. dried black-eyed peas
4 -5 C. water
1 1/2 tsp salt
1 C. fine egg noodles
1/2 C. chopped parsley
Meat:
1/2 lb ground beef

1/3 C. finely chopped onions or 1/3 C. grated onion
1/4 tsp cinnamon
1/4 tsp fine grind black pepper
1/2 tsp salt
Topping:
2 tsp dried mint
1/2 tsp black pepper
1/4 tsp cinnamon

Directions

1. Place a large pot of water over medium heat with a pinch of salt. Cook in it the beans with lentils for 38 min. Stir in the parsley with noodles.
2. Get a large mixing bowl: Combine in it the meatballs ingredients and mix them well. Shape the mix into meatballs. Add them to the pot and cook them for 35 min.
3. Get a mortar: Crush in it the mint with cinnamon and pepper. Sprinkle it over the soup then serve it warm.
4. Enjoy.

Persian
Eggplant Frittata

Prep Time: 15 mins
Total Time: 1 hr 20 mins

Servings per Recipe: 4
Calories	432.0
Fat	32.8g
Cholesterol	211.5mg
Sodium	766.5mg
Carbohydrates	27.5g
Protein	11.2g

Ingredients

2 large eggplants or 6 small eggplants, peeled and cut into thin strips
1 egg white, lightly beaten
1/2 C. vegetable oil, butter or 1/2 C. ghee
2 large onions, peeled and thinly sliced
4 garlic cloves, peeled and crushed
4 eggs
4 tbsp chopped fresh parsley
1/4 tsp powdered saffron, dissolved in 1

tbsp hot water
1 lime, juice of
1 tsp baking powder
1 tbsp all-purpose flour
1 tsp salt
1/4 tsp fresh ground black pepper

Directions

1. Remove the peel of the eggplants. Season them with some salt. Slice them into lengthwise. Brush both sides of the eggplant with the white egg.
2. Place a large pan over medium heat. Heat 4 tbsp of oil in it. Cook in it the onion for 12 min. Cook in it the garlic with eggplant for 12 min.
3. Before you do anything preheat the oven to 350 F.
4. Line up a baking dish with a parchment paper. Spread in the bottom of it 4 tbsp of vegetable oil.
5. Get a large mixing bowl: Whisk in it the eggs. Combine in it the parsley, saffron water, lime juice, baking powder, flour, salt, and pepper. Mix them well.
6. Combine the eggplant, onion and garlic. Stir them well. Cook them for 48 min. Serve your frittata warm.
7. Enjoy.

PERSIAN
Walnut Pomegranate Duck

🍲 Prep Time: 30 mins
🕐 Total Time: 1 hr 30 mins

Servings per Recipe: 4
Calories   1396.2
Fat   131.3g
Cholesterol   240.9mg
Sodium   204.6mg
Carbohydrates   13.9g
Protein   38.5g

Ingredients

1 duck, cut into quarters
2 onions, sliced
10 oz. finely chopped walnuts
2 1/2 C. water
salt and pepper, to taste
4 tbsp pomegranate syrup

2 tbsp sugar
2 tbsp lemon juice

Directions

1. Sprinkle some salt and pepper over the duck.
2. Place a large stew pot over medium heat. Melt in it the duck fat. Brown in it the duck pieces for 5 min. Add the onion and cook it for 3 min.
3. Remove the duck pieces from the pot and place them aside. Stir in the walnuts with 2 1/2 C. of water, a pinch of salt and pepper. Cook them for 1 min.
4. Stir in back the duck pieces. Cook them until they start boiling. Lower the heat and cook them for 1 h 10 min.
5. Get a small mixing bowl: Whisk in it the pomegranate syrup and sugar with the lemon juice. Spoon the fat from the rose on top and discard it.
6. Lower the heat and cook it for 32 min. Serve it warm.
7. Enjoy..

Persian
Almond Fruit Salad

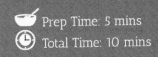

🥣 Prep Time: 5 mins

🕐 Total Time: 10 mins

Servings per Recipe: 6
Calories	442.5
Fat	12.7g
Cholesterol	0.0mg
Sodium	82.8mg
Carbohydrates	84.2g
Protein	8.1g

Ingredients

2 seedless oranges, peeled and cored

2 apples, peeled and cored

2 bananas, sliced

2 C. pitted dates, chopped

1 C. dried figs, chopped or 1 C. apricot

1 C. orange juice

1 C. almonds, chopped or 1 C. shredded coconut

Directions

1. Get a large mixing bowl: Stir in it the oranges with apples, bananas, dates and figs.
2. Pour the orange juice all over it and mix it well. Top it with almonds then place it in the fridge until ready to serve.
3. Enjoy..

PERSIAN
Cucumber Salad

🥣 Prep Time: 10 mins
🕐 Total Time: 20 mins

Servings per Recipe: 6
Calories	110.9
Fat	5.4g
Cholesterol	21.2mg
Sodium	77.2mg
Carbohydrates	10.3g
Protein	6.2g

Ingredients

32 fluid oz. plain yogurt
1/2 C. kefir cheese
1 large cucumber
2 tbsp mint (dried and crushed)
2 tbsp basil (fresh finely chopped)
1 tsp onion powder (optional)
2 tbsp dried rose petals (optional)

1/2 C. walnuts (crushed) (optional)
1/2 C. raisins (optional)
salt
1 tbsp black pepper, to taste

Directions

1. Get a large mixing bowl: Combine in it the yogurt and kefir cheese. Mix them well.
2. Peel the cucumbers and chop them finely. Stir in the basil, mint, salt, pepper, onion powder, raisins, walnuts, and dried rose petals. Place it in the fridge until ready to serve.
3. Enjoy.

Persian
Rosy Rice Pudding

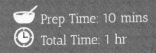

Prep Time: 10 mins
Total Time: 1 hr

Servings per Recipe: 4
Calories   1846.8
Fat   1.4g
Cholesterol   0.0mg
Sodium   5.1mg
Carbohydrates   443.9g
Protein   16.1g

Ingredients

500 g rice

1 kg sugar

cooking oil

1/2 tsp saffron

1/2 C. rose water

pistachios, crushed

almonds, crushed

1 tsp cinnamon

Directions

1. Rinse the rice with some water and drain it.
2. Place a large pot over medium heat. Place in it the rice and cover it with 6 times the amount of rice in water. Cook the rice until it is done.
3. Stir in the sugar until it completely melts.
4. Pour half C. of water in a small bowl. Stir in it the saffron then add it to the pot.
5. Pour the oil in a small saucepan. Heat it through and add it to the pot. Stir in the rosewater with almonds.
6. Lower the heat and cook the rice pudding for 30 min. Serve it warm with your favorite toppings.
7. Enjoy.

FENUGREEK
Lamb Stew

🍲 Prep Time: 20 mins
🕐 Total Time: 2 hrs 50 mins

Servings per Recipe: 6
Calories	356.9
Fat	20.4g
Cholesterol	98.4mg
Sodium	207.4mg
Carbohydrates	9.0g
Protein	33.2g

Ingredients

2 lbs boneless lamb stewing meat (cut into 3/4-inch cubes) or 2 lbs boneless beef roast (cut into 3/4-inch cubes)
1 large onion, finely chopped
1/3 C. cooking oil
1 tsp turmeric
1 1/2 C. water
6 dried limes or 1/2 C. fresh lime juice
3/4 C. kidney bean
1 large potato, diced (optional)

salt
black pepper
1 C. green onion, finely chopped
1 1/2 C. spinach, finely chopped
1/2 C. parsley, finely chopped
1/4 C. cilantro, finely chopped (optional)
1/4 C. garlic chives, finely chopped
1/4 C. fenugreek seeds, finely chopped (optional)

Directions

1. Discard the excess fat for the lamb and cut it into dices.
2. Place a large pan over medium heat. Heat in it half of the oil. Sauté in it the onion for 3 min. Add the lamb dices and cook them for 2 min.
3. Lower the heat then stir in the water, drained kidney beans, salt and pepper. Put on the lid and cook them for 1 h 10 min.
4. Place a large skillet over medium heat. Heat the rest of the oil in it. Add the potato and cook it until it becomes golden brown.
5. Drain the potato and stir it into the stew. Put on the lid and cook them for 12 min.
6. Add the remaining veggies into the same skillet and cook them for 4 min. Stir the mix with dry lime into the stew.
7. Put on the lid and cook the stew for 14 min. Serve it warm.
8. Enjoy..

Persian
Cinnamon Parsley Beef Stew

Prep Time: 25 mins
Total Time: 1 hr 40 mins

Servings per Recipe: 4
Calories   425.1
Fat   24.3g
Cholesterol   82.9mg
Sodium   388.7mg
Carbohydrates   21.3g
Protein   30.0g

Ingredients

3 tbsp olive oil, divided (2 tbsp. and 1 tbsp.)

1/2 large onion, chopped

1 lb lean stewing beef, cubed

2 tsp ground cumin

2 tsp ground turmeric

1/2 tsp ground cinnamon

2 1/2 C. water

5 tbsp fresh flat-leaf parsley, chopped

3 tbsp snipped chives

1 (15 oz.) cans kidney beans, drained and rinsed

1 lemon, juice of

1 tbsp flour

salt and black pepper

Directions

1. Place a large pan over medium heat. Heat 2 tbsp of olive oil in it. Brown in it the stew meat for 12 min.
2. Stir in the cumin, turmeric and cinnamon. Cook them for 2 min. Pour in the water and cook them until they start boiling.
3. Put on the lid and cook them for 48 min while stirring from to time.
4. Place a small skillet over medium heat. Heat 1 tbsp of oil in it. Add the parsley with chives. Cook them for 3 min. Stir them into the beef stew with beans and lemon juice.
5. Sprinkle some salt and pepper on the stew then add to it 1 tbsp of flour. Cook the stew for 35 min until it thickens. Serve it warm.
6. Enjoy..

LEMON
Lamb Kabobs

🥣 Prep Time: 10 mins
🕐 Total Time: 30 mins

Servings per Recipe: 12
Calories	94.9
Fat	5.8g
Cholesterol	25.7mg
Sodium	235.6mg
Carbohydrates	2.7g
Protein	7.4g

Ingredients

1 lb ground beef or 1 lb lamb

1 medium onion, grated

1/4 C. breadcrumbs or 1/4 C. white flour

1 egg, slightly beaten (optional)

1 tsp turmeric

1 tsp salt

1/2 tsp pepper

1 tbsp lemon juice

Directions

1. Squeeze the onion for the liquid. Transfer it to a large mixing bowl with the rest of the ingredients. Mix them well and place them in the fridge.
2. Preheat a grill and grease its grates.
3. Shape the mix into 10 or 12 patties. Press them into skewers to make logs. Cook the kabobs on the grill for 6 to 8 min on each side. Serve them warm.
4. Enjoy.

Persian Potato Lamb Stew

Prep Time: 30 mins
Total Time: 1 hr 40 mins

Servings per Recipe: 4

Calories	551.6
Fat	23.8g
Cholesterol	90.5mg
Sodium	1341.5mg
Carbohydrates	64.1g
Protein	25.8g

Ingredients

1 lb lamb, cut in cubes (or beef)

1/4 C. butter

1 lb green beans, cut in one-inch pieces

1 C. tomato paste

1 lb carrot, cut in one-inch slices

2 large waxy potatoes, cut in one-inch cubes

1/2 tsp cinnamon

1 tsp salt

1/4 tsp black pepper

1 tsp turmeric

Directions

1. Season the lamb meat with cinnamon.
2. Place a large pan over medium heat. Melt the butter in it. Cook in it the meat in batches for 5 min per batch. Stir in 2 C. of water.
3. Cook them until they start boiling. Lower the heat and cook them for 38 min with the lid on. Stir in the green beans, tomato paste, carrots, potatoes and spices.
4. Cook them for 38 min with the lid on. Adjust the seasoning of the stew then serve it warm.
5. Enjoy.

PERSIAN
Honey Fish Filets

Prep Time: 15 mins
Total Time: 35 mins

Servings per Recipe: 3
Calories   289.7
Fat   2.2g
Cholesterol   132.0mg
Sodium   302.8mg
Carbohydrates   10.0g
Protein   56.0g

Ingredients

1/8 C. pomegranate molasses
1/3 C. water
1/2 C. tomato juice
1 lemon, juice of
1/2 tsp lemon zest
1/8 C. freshly squeezed lime juice
sea salt, to taste
1/8 tsp cumin
1/8 tsp cinnamon
1/8 tsp ground cardamom
couple pinches allspice

1/2 tbsp honey
olive oil
1/2 bunch scallion, chopped
1 garlic clove, crushed
4 fish fillets
gluten-free flour, mix

Directions

1. Get a small mixing bowl: Whisk in it the pomegranate molasses and water, tomato juice, lemon juice and zest, lime juice, sea salt, spices, and honey.
2. Place a large saucepan over medium heat. Heat 2 tbsp of olive oil in it. Sauté in it the garlic with scallions. Cook them for 3 min.
3. Stir in the molasses mix. Cook them until it starts boiling. Cook them for 4 min. Place the mix aside to make the sauce.
4. Before you do anything preheat the oven to 450 F.
5. Season the fish fillets with some salt. Dust the flour with them.
6. Place a large skillet over medium heat. Heat a splash of oil in it. Cook in it the fish fillets until they becomes golden brown for 3 to 6 min on each side.
7. Lay the fish fillets in a greased baking dish. Drizzle the sauce all over them. Cook them in the oven for 10 min. Serve your fish warm.
8. Enjoy.

Persian
Okra Lime Stew

Prep Time: 15 mins
Total Time: 1 hr 40 mins

Servings per Recipe: 4
Calories   400.7
Fat   12.2g
Cholesterol   147.4mg
Sodium   259.5mg
Carbohydrates   22.3g
Protein   50.7g

Ingredients

1 1/2 lbs fresh okra

2 - 3 garlic cloves, sliced

2 lbs stewing lamb or 2 lbs beef, cut into small pieces

1 lb potato (optional)

2 large onions, sliced

2 - 3 tbsp fresh lime juice

3 - 4 tbsp tomato paste

cooking oil

salt and black pepper

Directions

1. Cut the onion into thin slices.
2. Place a large pan over medium heat. Heat a splash of oil in it. Add the onion and cook it until it becomes golden. Add the lamb dices with garlic.
3. Cook them for 3 min. Stir 3 C. of hot water. Cook them until they start boiling. Lower the heat and put on the lid. Cook them for 48 min.
4. Clean the okra and discard its stems. Add it to the pan with tomato paste, a pinch of salt and pepper. Put on the lid and cook it for 16 min without stirring.
5. Stir in the lime juice. Adjust the seasoning of the stew then serve it warm.
6. Enjoy.

PERSIAN
Basmati Casserole

Prep Time: 2 hrs 15 mins

Total Time: 4 hrs 40 mins

Servings per Recipe: 4
Calories	865.3
Fat	29.9g
Cholesterol	259.5mg
Sodium	183.4mg
Carbohydrates	101.6g
Protein	44.8g

Ingredients
1 (2 1/4 lb) whole chicken
1 lb basmati rice
10 oz. plain nonfat yogurt
1/2 tsp saffron
2 large onions

3 egg yolks
cooking oil
salt (to taste)
black pepper (to taste)

Directions
1. Get a large bowl: Place in it the rice and cover it with warm water. Place it aside for 2 h 15 min.
2. Cut the chicken into pieces. Discard its skin. Peel the onion and chop it.
3. Place a large pan over medium heat. Heat a splash of oil in it. Sauté in it the onion for 3 min. Add the chicken and brown it.
4. Stir in some water and cook them until they start boiling. Lower the heat and cook them until the chicken is done while adding water if needed. Shred it
5. Get a large mixing bowl: Pour in it the yogurt. Beat it until it becomes creamy. Place it aside.
6. Get half C. of hot water. Stir in it the saffron until it dissolves. Add it to the yogurt with salt, pepper and egg yolks. Combine them well.
7. Cook the rice according to the directions on the package.
8. Before you do anything preheat the oven to 250 F.
9. Coat the bottom of a dutch oven with 3 tbsp of vegetable oil. Spread in it a thin layer of the yogurt mix followed by a thin layer of rice, chicken, another layer of rice and yogurt.
10. Repeat the process to make several other layers. Place the pot in the oven and cook it for 1 h 50 min.
11. Serve your chicken rice casserole warm.
12. Enjoy.

Persian
Lemon Linguini

Prep Time: 20 mins
Total Time: 40 mins

Servings per Recipe: 4
Calories	816.4
Fat	33.4g
Cholesterol	53.6mg
Sodium	812.7mg
Carbohydrates	99.4g
Protein	28.9g

Ingredients

500 g linguine
2 garlic cloves, peeled
2 tsp lemon rind, finely grated
1 bunch fresh basil, leaves picked
1/3 C. olive oil
3 anchovy fillets

flaked sea salt
black pepper, freshly ground
1/4 C. lemon juice
1/2 C. parmesan cheese, finely grated
2 egg tomatoes, finely chopped
180 g feta, drained, crumbled

Directions

1. Prepare the pasta by following the instructions on the package.
2. Get a mortar: Combine in it the garlic, lemon rind, half the basil and half the oil. Crush them with the pestle. Combine in the anchovies with the rest of basil.
3. Crush them again with the pestle. Stir in a pinch of salt and pepper.
4. Get a large mixing bowl: Toss in it the pasta with garlic mix, lemon juice and parmesan. Stir in the feta with tomato. Serve your pasta warm.
5. Enjoy.

PERSIAN
6-Ingredient Rice

Prep Time: 15 mins
Total Time: 1 hr

Servings per Recipe: 8
Calories   342.5
Fat   9.9g
Cholesterol   20.3mg
Sodium   89.8mg
Carbohydrates   57.2g
Protein   6.8g

Ingredients

3 C. long grain white basmati rice
2 bunches green onions, minced
1 C. fresh dill weed, finely chopped
1 C. fresh parsley, finely chopped
1 C. fresh cilantro, finely chopped
1/3 C. butter)

Directions

1. Get a large bowl: Place in it the rice and cover it with warm water. Place it aside for 2 h 15 min.
2. Fill half a large pot with water and a pinch of salt. Cook it until it starts boiling. Add the rice and cook it until it starts boiling.
3. Keep cooking it for 9 min. Strain the rice and place it aside to drain.
4. Get a food processor: Combine the scallions, dill, parsley and cilantro. Process them until they becomes smooth.
5. Melt the butter in a large pot over medium heat. Lay in it 1/3 of the cooked rice followed by half of the herbs mix. Repeat the process to make 2 other layers.
6. Make 5 holes with the spatula handle in the rice. Place a piece of foil over the pot and place the lid on it. Place it over medium heat and cook it for 4 min.
7. Lower the heat and cook it for 38 min. Place it aside for 16 min to rest. Serve it warm.
8. Enjoy.

Persian
Kashk Lamb Meatballs
Stew

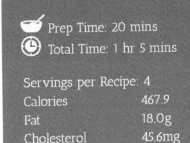

Prep Time: 20 mins
Total Time: 1 hr 5 mins

Servings per Recipe: 4
Calories	467.9
Fat	18.0g
Cholesterol	45.6mg
Sodium	324.7mg
Carbohydrates	53.2g
Protein	33.7g

Ingredients

250 g ground lamb or 250 g beef
50 g dried black-eye beans
50 g dried split peas
50 g dried brown lentils
1 kg fresh spinach
2 onions
100 g of fresh mint

1/4 tsp pomegranate powder
1 C. kashk
vegetable oil
salt
black pepper

Directions

1. Rinse the black-eye beans, split-peas, and lentils. Place them in a large bowl and cover them with water. Place them aside to soak for 4 h 10 min.
2. Rinse them and drain them. Place them in large saucepan with 4 1/4 C. of water with a pinch of salt. Cook them for 22 min over medium heat until 1 C. of liquid is left.
3. Get a large mixing bowl: Grate the onion and add to it the lamb with a pinch of salt and pepper. Mix them well. Shape the mix into meatballs.
4. Place a large pan over medium heat. Heat a splash of oil in it. Brown in it the meatballs for 4 min.
5. Rinse the spinach with some cool water and chop them. Stir them into the saucepan with the beans mix and meatballs. Cook them for 18 min. Stir in the pomegranate powder.
6. Place a small skillet over medium heat. Heat a splash of oil in it. Add the mint and fry it. Crush it and use it to garnish the stew. Serve it warm.
7. Enjoy.

PERSIAN
Sesame Bread

🥣 Prep Time: 1 hr 15 mins

🕐 Total Time: 1 hr 45 mins

Servings per Recipe: 1 loaf
Calories	2450.9
Fat	61.9 g
Cholesterol	0.0 mg
Sodium	2372.2 mg
Carbohydrates	410.2 g
Protein	58.9 g

Ingredients

500 g flour

40 g fresh yeast

250 - 275 ml warm water

1 tbsp brown sugar

1 tsp salt

4 tbsp olive oil

2 tbsp corn flour (optional)

1 tsp black sesame

Directions

1. Get a large mixing bowl: Mix in it the flour with corn flour and a pinch of salt. Mix them well.

2. Make a small well in the middle of the flour mix. Place in it the sugar with yeast and 5 tbsp of warm water Mix them well. Place it a side with a kitchen towel to cover it for 28 min.

3. Add the rest of the water and water then mix them again until you get a smooth dough. Place it aside to rest for 1 h 10 min.

4. Before you do anything preheat the oven to 400 F.

5. Shape the dough into several circles of flat bread and place them on lined up baking sheet. Brush them with olive oil and top them with sesame seeds.

6. Cook them in the oven for 15 to 18 min. Serve it warm or cold.

7. Enjoy.

Persian Skillet:
Chicken Apricots Stir Fry

🥄 Prep Time: 15 mins
🕐 Total Time: 35 mins

Servings per Recipe: 4
Calories	588.6
Fat	27.1g
Cholesterol	72.6mg
Sodium	398.9mg
Carbohydrates	59.9g
Protein	33.6g

Ingredients

1 lb chicken breast, cut into 2 inch cubes
oil (for frying)
4 large portabella mushrooms, cut into 2 inch cubes
4 oz. dried apricots, coarsely chopped
1 C. cashews
3/4 C. raisins
salt and pepper
1/2 C. chicken broth
1 tbsp brown sugar
2 tsp sweet paprika
1/2 tsp ground ginger

Directions

1. Place a large pan over medium heat. Heat a splash of oil in it. Add the chicken and brown it for 5 min.
2. Stir in the mushroom and cook them for 3 min. Stir in the apricots, raisins, brown sugar, paprika, ginger, and salt and pepper. Cook them for 1 min 4 min.
3. Stir in the broth and cook them for 6 min over high heat. Fold in the cashews. Serve your stir fry with some rice.
4. Enjoy.

LEBANESE
Fattoush
(Levantine Bread Salad)

Servings per Recipe: 4
Calories	305 kcal
Carbohydrates	29.1 g
Cholesterol	0 mg
Fat	19.9 g
Fiber	5.5 g
Protein	6 g
Sodium	294 mg

Ingredients

2 pita breads, cut into two half pieces
1 head romaine lettuce, chopped
2 tomatoes, diced
2 green onions, thinly sliced
1 cucumber, diced
1 cup sliced green olives
4 radishes, sliced
1 green or red bell pepper, chopped

1/4 cup chopped fresh mint
2 tbsps sumac
1 tbsp salt, or (your preferred amount)
1/4 cup fresh lemon juice
1/4 cup olive oil

Directions

1. Set your oven to 425 degrees before doing anything else.
2. Put pita in a baking dish.
3. Bake pita for 5 mins in the oven.
4. Remove the baking dish and set it to the side for cooling.
5. Now break the pita into small pieces.
6. Grab the following ingredients: green peppers, lettuce, radishes, tomatoes, olives, onions, cucumber and the baked pita pieces.
7. Put all of the ingredients into a salad bowl and add: salt, mint, and sumac.
8. Toss evenly.
9. Add some olive oil and lemon juice. Chill the salad in the fridge.
10. Enjoy.

Donair
Meat Kabobs
(Lebanese Style)

🥣 Prep Time: 40 mins

🕐 Total Time: 5 hrs 35 mins

Servings per Recipe: 7

Calories	990 kcal
Carbohydrates	47.6 g
Cholesterol	128 mg
Fat	64.7 g
Fiber	6.8 g
Protein	57.5 g
Sodium	426 mg

Ingredients

3 1/4 lbs boneless top round steak, sliced very thin
1/2 cup red wine vinegar
1/2 cup olive oil
1/4 cup fresh lemon juice
1 tsp allspice
1/2 tsp ground cinnamon
1/4 tsp cardamom
1/2 tsp ground black pepper
salt, (your preferred amount)
2 large tomatoes, coarsely chopped
1 clove garlic, minced
Parsley Sauce:
1 bunch finely chopped fresh parsley

1 large sweet onion, finely chopped
1/3 cup olive oil
3 tbsps fresh lemon juice
3 large tomatoes, coarsely chopped
Tahini Sauce:
2 cloves garlic, minced
1 cup tahini (sesame-seed paste)
1/2 cup fresh lemon juice
1/2 cup water
salt (your taste)
7 pita bread rounds

Directions

1. Grab a dish ready for baking. Take your beef and place it on the dish.
2. Get the following items: garlic, red wine vinegar, tomatoes, half a cup of olive oil, salt, juiced lemon, pepper, allspice, cardamom, and cinnamon.
3. Put all contents into a big container (possibly a bowl) and mix together.
4. Take your seasoning and cover your beef with it. Making sure each piece is covered evenly.
5. Place a lid on your seasoned beef and place everything into the fridge for about four hours to marinate. More time is better.
6. Now let's get the oven ready. Turn it on to 425 degrees Fahrenheit.
7. Once the oven is 425 degrees. Grab your dish, take off its lid, and place it into the oven to cook until you notice all the beef is done. This will take about 50 minutes.
8. Take out the meat and set it to the side for cooling.
9. Now it's time to make our parsley covering.

10.Grab the following items: half a cup of olive oil, parsley, and sweet onions and put all the contents together into a big container for mixing.

11. Combine with the oil, some tomatoes, and put the mixture to the side to rest for a bit.

12. Now we need to get another dish to make our tahini.

13. So get another dish and combine the following items: water, garlic, juiced lemon, tahini, and your preferred amount of salt.

14. Now we are ready to serve our food.

15. Grab some pita bread and roll its sides upwards.

16. Put some meat mixture into the pita, with a layer of parsley covering over the top, and finally another layer of tahini.

17. Place the filled roll on a plate.

18. Serve and enjoy.

Lebanese
Bean Salad

Prep Time: 10 mins
Total Time: 2 hrs 20 mins

Servings per Recipe: 5
Calories	312 kcal
Carbohydrates	44.7 g
Cholesterol	0 mg
Fat	9.3 g
Fiber	10 g
Protein	13.2 g
Sodium	418 mg

Ingredients

1 (15 ounce) can fava beans, drained and rinsed

1 (15 ounce) can chickpeas, drained and rinsed

1 (15.5 ounce) can white beans, drained and rinsed

1/4 cup chopped flat leaf parsley, or more (your preferred amount)

3 tbsps olive oil

2 cloves garlic, minced

1 lemon, juiced

kosher salt and ground black pepper (your preferred amount)

Directions

1. To make this recipe let's start with a large dish for mixing (possibly a bowl) and place into our container the following items: juiced lemon, fava beans, garlic, chickpeas, olive oil, white beans, and some parsley.
2. Combine with the mixture some black pepper and some salt.
3. Put the container in the fridge for about two hrs to let everything marinate and cool off.
4. Plate, enjoy.

LEBANESE
Rice Pilaf

Prep Time: 20 mins
Total Time: 55 mins

Servings per Recipe: 6 cups
Calories	203 kcal
Carbohydrates	18 g
Cholesterol	20 mg
Fat	13.4 g
Fiber	0.8 g
Protein	2.8 g
Sodium	641 mg

Ingredients

3 cups parboiled long-grain white rice
1/2 cup butter, divided
1/4 cup olive oil, divided
1/2 cup orzo pasta
4 cups water
1 tbsp salt

1 tbsp slivered almonds, or (your preferred amount)
1 tbsp tahini

Directions

1. First we need to get a nice sized container for our rice.
2. Fill the container with water and place the rice into it.
3. Let everything relax for about 10 mins. Now remove the rice from the water and run cool water over the rice until you notice the water running clear.
4. Grab a frying pan or skillet and heat the pan with a medium level of heat.
5. Add 2 tbsps of olive oil with one fourth cup of butter to the pan and mix into the oils some orzo.
6. Fry your orzo down until you notice it becoming a nice brownish color. This will take about five mins.
7. Now that the orzo is brown let's grab our rice and increase the level of heat slightly (should be high at this point).
8. For 5 mins we want to mix into the oil orzo mixture all the rice and continue cooking until we notice that the rice kernels are translucent.
9. Grab some water and cover the rice with it.
10. Combine with the water and rice some salt and get everything to a boiling point.
11. Grab a lid and cover the rice. Make sure you turn the heat down to its lowest level and let the rice cook until it becomes fluffy. Make sure to not open the pot while the rice is

cooking (we need the pressure to build up inside the pot).

12. Continue cooking your rice for about 20 mins.
13. Now grab another frying pan or skillet and get some olive oil hot. Heating level should be medium.
14. Add some almonds to the oil mix and fry them until they are nice and toasted. You will eventually notice a nice fragrance from the cooked almonds.
15. Overall the almond frying process should take about 5 mins.
16. Finally we want to add some butter and tahini to the almonds and evenly cover each almond with the mixture.
17. Combine the almond mixture with the rice and plate the contents.
18. Enjoy..

KIBBEE
Lebanese Beef Croquettes

🥣 Prep Time: 20 mins
🕐 Total Time: 50 mins

Servings per Recipe: 4

Calories	417 kcal
Carbohydrates	16.8 g
Cholesterol	83 mg
Fat	29 g
Fiber	4 g
Protein	22.4 g
Sodium	219 mg

Ingredients

1/2 cup bulgur
1/2 cup hot water
1/2 tsp dried mint
1/4 tsp ground allspice
1/4 tsp ground black pepper
1/8 tsp ground cinnamon

1/4 tsp salt
1 onion, minced
2 tbsps chopped fresh parsley
1 lb ground lamb, or beef
2 tbsps pine nuts

Directions

1. Let's start this recipe by getting our ovens ready for some work. So turn on the oven to 350 degrees Fahrenheit or 175 degrees Celsius.
2. Now we need a square container for baking. Preferably this dish should be about 8 inches.
3. Grab your bulgur and place it into a container for soaking.
4. Place some water that's hot into a container and place your bulgur into the water letting it sit for about 10 minutes. At this point you should notice the bulgur expanding.
5. Now let's get our food processor and get it ready for some work too.
6. Take the following items and put them into the processor: lamb, bulgur, parsley, mint, onions, allspice, salt, pepper, and cinnamon.
7. Process everything for about one min to make sure it's nice and smooth.
8. Grab your baking dish from before and split the lamb mix in half on the dish and make a big patty.
9. Put some pine nuts over the lamb and then take the remaining lamb meat and cover the pine nuts with the meat. Make sure to compress the patty layers nicely.
10. Get your kibbee and dice it into one and a half inch squares.
11. Place the lamb into the oven for about 35 mins.
12. At this point you should not see any pinkness in the meat.
13. If you have a thermometer the temperature readout should be 160 degrees Fahrenheit or 70 Celsius.
14. Plate and enjoy.

Lebanese
Semolina Cookies

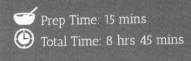

Prep Time: 15 mins
Total Time: 8 hrs 45 mins

Servings per Recipe: 15
Calories	414 kcal
Carbohydrates	73.6 g
Cholesterol	57 mg
Fat	10.5 g
Fiber	0.9 g
Protein	8.2 g
Sodium	80 mg

Ingredients
Pudding:

8 cups cold milk

1 1/2 cups semolina

2 eggs

3 tbsps rose water

Glaze:

4 cups white sugar

2 1/4 cups water

1/4 tsp lemon juice

Garnish:

1 cup whipping cream

1 tbsp white sugar

1/3 cup finely chopped pistachio nuts

Directions
1. Let's begin by grabbing a nice large pan. Put your milk into the pan and heat everything over a medium level of heat. Continue heating your milk until it is boiling.
2. Once the milk is boiling we want to turn down the heat and begin to mix in our semolina at a slow but consistent rate. Take care to stir consistently.
3. Now keep stirring for about one to two mins. The milk should still be boiling while stirring and after one to 2 mins you should notice the contents have become thick.
4. Now we want to remove the pan from the heat.
5. Combine your eggs and rose water into the milk taking care to stir continually. Now you can either grab one larger serving dish or multiple dishes.
6. Put some mixture into each dish or into your one large dish. Let the contents cool for a bit and cover the dish(es). Now we want to put the contents into the fridge for at least five hrs (but overnight is ideal).
7. Now grab another pan and pour some water and sugar into it to begin the syrup creation process.
8. Heat the pan over a medium level of heat and continually stir the contents allowing the sugar to dissipate.
9. Continue cooking and stirring until you find the contents are a brownish golden color.
10. Once the desired color has been achieved remove the pan from its heating source and add

the remaining water and stir it in. If your contents get harder do not worry.

11. Put the pan back on its heating source and add the rest of the sugar and get it to dissipate. Now we want to combine some juiced lemon with the mixture and continue applying heat until everything is boiling.

12. Let the mixture boil / simmer for about ten mins. After 10 mins of boiling take the pan away from its heating source. Place a lid over the pan and set it aside to cool. This syrup is good for a month if covered and keep cool.

13. Now before we serve this dish we want to take some whip cream and combine it with some sugar and whip it until it hardens a bit.

14. Take this whipped cream with sugar and place it over the pudding mixture and put some nuts on top of it.

15. The pudding should be diced into squares and covered with some caramel syrup for best taste.

16. Enjoy

Lebanese
Seven Spices

🥣 Prep Time: 5 mins
🕐 Total Time: 10 mins

Servings per Recipe: 15
Calories	7 kcal
Carbohydrates	1.2 g
Cholesterol	0 mg
Fat	0.3 g
Fiber	0.7 g
Protein	0.3 g
Sodium	2 mg

Ingredients

1/2 cup ground black pepper

1/2 cup ground cumin

1/2 cup paprika

1/4 cup ground coriander

1/4 cup ground cloves

4 tsps ground nutmeg

4 tsps ground cinnamon

2 tsps ground cardamom

Directions

1. Making this amazing spice is quite easy so let's begin by grabbing a container for storage.
2. Put the following ingredients into the container: cardamom, black pepper, cinnamon, cumin, nutmeg, paprika, clove, and coriander.
3. Make sure to mix the spices together nicely.
4. Cover the container with a good lid so no air can penetrate.
5. Store and enjoy.

LEBANESE
Cardamom Clove Cookies

 Prep Time: 2 hrs
Total Time: 10 hrs 10 mins

Servings per Recipe: 60 cookies	
Calories	289 kcal
Carbohydrates	44.6 g
Cholesterol	24 mg
Fat	10 g
Fiber	1.6 g
Protein	5.2 g
Sodium	67 mg

Ingredients

1 1/2 lbs butter
4 cups white sugar
1 cup water
9 cups semolina flour
8 cups all-purpose flour
1 1/2 tbsps quick rise yeast
1 tsp ground cinnamon
1/2 tsp freshly grated nutmeg

1/2 tsp ground cloves
1/2 tsp ground cardamom
1/2 tsp allspice
1 tsp ground mahleb
1/4 cup black sesame seeds
1/4 cup rose water
1/4 cup orange flower water
1 cup warm water

Directions

1. Let's begin by grabbing a pan and heating it with a low level of heat.
2. Grab some butter and melt it down nicely.
3. Combine some sugar and water with the butter and take care to stir it continually.
4. But make sure that you prevent the mixture from reaching a boiling state.
5. Get everything combined nicely and take it away from its heating source and allow it to cool.
6. Grab a container (possibly a bowl) and put in your flour and the following items: sesame seeds, melted butter, spices, and yeast.
7. Combine the items for about 10 mins by stirring.
8. Let the dough sit about an hour. Make sure you cover your container.
9. Now we need to get three baking dishes and get them ready for some work.
10. Spray each dish with non stick cooking spray.
11. Grab another small container or bowl and mix in your orange flower and rose water. Grab an additional bowl and fill it with some water that is warm.

12. Now we want to move everything to a flat surface that is covered in flour and begin to remove approx. one cup of dough from the dough container.

13. You now want to cover your fingers in the warm water and knead the dough for one min.

14. After kneading the dough for a min dunk it into the flower water and continue to knead it. You should notice the dough is nice and soft eventually.

15. Roll the soft dough into a foot long rope like shape that should be about one inch deep.

16. Halve the dough into two pieces and form it into a wreath like shape (basically a circle).

17. Press the ends of each piece together. Take your soon to be cookies and place them on a baking dish.

18. Continue to make cookies like this until you have filled a baking dish.

19. Once the dish is full place it in the fridge over night. The dish should be covered with a towel.

20. After the dough has set for a night get your oven ready for work by bringing it to 350 degrees Fahrenheit or 175 degrees Celsius.

21. Before entering your cookies into the oven let them warm up to room temperature. Once at room temperature and the oven is nice and preheated place the cookies into the oven for about 15 mins. After 15 mins the cookies will be nice and brown.

22. Remove the cookies from the oven.

23. Let cool. Serve. Enjoy.

LEBANESE
Radish Salad

Prep Time: 20 mins
Total Time: 35 mins

Servings per Recipe: 4 cups
Calories   155 kcal
Carbohydrates   4.5 g
Cholesterol   0 mg
Fat   14.9 g
Fiber   1.9 g
Protein   2.7 g
Sodium   202 mg

Ingredients

1 cup walnut halves

1 lb radishes, trimmed and sliced into thin rounds

3 tbsps extra-virgin olive oil

2 tsps fresh lemon juice

3/4 tsp kosher salt

1/2 tsp honey

20 fresh mint leaves

Directions

1. To make this salad we first need to grab a frying pan or skillet. Get the pan nice and hot with a medium level of heat and throw into the pan your walnuts.
2. Cook the walnuts until they are toasted and you smell their nice fragrance. You'll notice the colour of the walnuts change to a darker one when they are ready for the next step. This should take about 4 mins.
3. Once the walnuts are toasted, we want to dice them nicely.
4. Grab a container and place into it some radishes.
5. Grab another container (but smaller) and place the following it: honey, oil, salt, and juiced lemons.
6. Mix the contents together in the small bowl. Take this mixture and cover the radishes with it evenly. You may want to toss the radishes to get your even coating.
7. Now we want to grab some mint leaves and place them on top of each other in layers on the counter. Once layered, roll them up, and cut them to create a ribbon like shape.
8. Take your mint ribbons and combine them with the radishes and the walnuts.
9. Serve as is. Enjoy.

Lebanese Baked Eggplants

Prep Time: 20 mins
Total Time: 1 h 30 mins

Servings per Recipe: 6

Calories	615 kcal
Carbohydrates	42.5 g
Cholesterol	66 mg
Fat	39.1 g
Fiber	9.3 g
Protein	29.2 g
Sodium	745 mg

Ingredients

2 eggplants

1 tsp salt

2 tbsps olive oil

1 lb beef stew meat, cut into small pieces

1 large onion, chopped

1 1/2 cups chopped walnuts

2 large potatoes, cut into 1 inch cubes

2 (14.5 ounce) cans stewed tomatoes

salt and pepper (your preferred amount)

Directions

1. Let's begin by grabbing our eggplants and cutting them up into .5 inch rectangular slices.
2. Take one tsp of salt and season the eggplants. Once the eggplants have been salted let them sit for 20 mins.
3. Take care to remove any liquid which drains off the eggplants with a paper towel.
4. Now let's get our oven ready by turning it to 350 degrees Fahrenheit or 175 degrees Celsius.
5. While our ovens are heating, grab a frying pan or skillet and heat it over a medium level of heat.
6. Put some olive oil in the pan and let it get hot.
7. Combine the meat and onions in the oil and get everything nice and brown. Once everything is brown add the walnuts to the mix and let it cook for about 2 more mins. After two min take the pan away from its heating source.
8. Grab a dish, safe for baking, and place half of the eggplant pieces into it. Now we want to take our meat and layer it over the eggplant.
9. Grab the rest of the eggplant and put it on top of the meat.
10. Now on top of this layer of meat we want to add a layer of the following mixture: tomatoes, potatoes, pepper, and salt.
11. Place the layered items into the oven and let it bake for about one hour. At this point you should find that your eggplant is soft. The food is now ready for consumption.
12. Let everything cool. Plate. Enjoy.

LEBANESE
Lemon Lentil Soup

 Prep Time: 30 mins

Total Time: 2 hrs 5 mins

Servings per Recipe: 10
Calories	268 kcal
Carbohydrates	37.8 g
Cholesterol	12 mg
Fat	8.2 g
Fiber	13.9 g
Protein	12 g
Sodium	755 mg

Ingredients

2 tbsps olive oil

1 large yellow onion, diced

2 stalks celery with leaves, diced

2 carrots, diced

1 1/2 tsps minced garlic

6 cups water

2 cups French green lentils

2 tbsps chopped fresh parsley

1 tbsp salt, or more (your preferred amount)

1 tbsp ground coriander

1 tbsp ground cumin

1 1/2 tsps ground black pepper

1/2 tsp cayenne pepper

1/4 cup butter (optional)

1 cup all-purpose flour (optional)

1 lemon, cut into wedges

2 tbsps chopped fresh parsley

freshly ground black pepper

Directions

1. Begin this delicious recipe by getting a cooking pot. Put some olive oil into the pot and heat everything over a medium level of heat.

2. Stir fry the following items: carrots, onion, and celery. We should stir fry the items for five mins until you notice they have become soft. Once soft add some garlic.

3. For about 30 secs continue to fry everything until you notice a pleasant fragrance.

4. Add some water to the mix and the following items: cayenne pepper, lentils, cumin, 2 tbsps of parsley (fresh), black pepper, salt, and coriander. Make sure to continually stir the contents as you add everything to the mix.

5. Cover your new mixture and get it to a simmering point. Take care to stir everything once and a while.

6. Lower the heat and let the contents cook down for about one and a half hours. At this point you should notice you lentils have become soft.

7. Now grab another pan.

8. Combine flour and butter while whisking for 10 mins. The heat level should be medium to low. You want to continue whisking until the mixture becomes like a paste.

9. Once you have created a paste like mixture lower the heat to its lowest setting. Take care to stir the contents every two or three mins.

10. Continue to cook on low heat until the paste becomes brown. This should take about 20 mins.

11. Now take the paste and mix it into the new mixture by spoon. Taking care whisk each spoonful gracefully into the soup for best taste.

12. You'll eventually create a creamy rich soup with this method.

13. Once creamy and all the flour has been added to the soup it is ready to be served with the following items: freshly ground pepper, lemon wedges, and 2 tbsps of parsley (fresh preferably).

14. Enjoy.

LEBANESE
Lemon Salad Dressing

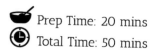 Prep Time: 20 mins
Total Time: 50 mins

Servings per Recipe: 1 cup
Calories	176 kcal
Carbohydrates	2.4 g
Cholesterol	0 mg
Fat	18.7 g
Fiber	0.2 g
Protein	0.2 g
Sodium	321 mg

Ingredients

1/2 cup fresh lemon juice
1/2 cup mild extra-virgin olive oil
3 cloves garlic, minced
1 tsp kosher salt
ground black pepper (your preferred amount)

Directions

1. This is a very simple, but tasty dressing so let's get started by grabbing a nice sized container for storage (preferably a bowl).
2. Now combine your items: pepper, juiced lemon, salt, olive oil, and garlic.
3. Take care to mix everything nicely.
4. Serve immediately as dressing for all types of salads.
5. Enjoy.

Tabouli
Levantine Parsley Salad

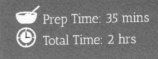 Prep Time: 35 mins
Total Time: 2 hrs

Servings per Recipe: 8
Calories	182 kcal
Carbohydrates	14.1 g
Cholesterol	0 mg
Fat	14 g
Fiber	3.5 g
Protein	2.7 g
Sodium	889 mg

Ingredients

2/3 cup water

1/3 cup bulgur

1 tbsp salt

1/2 cup fresh lemon juice

1/2 cup olive oil

1 3/4 lbs tomatoes, chopped

2 onions, finely chopped

2 bunches fresh parsley, chopped

1 bunch fresh mint, chopped

Directions

1. Begin with a pot. Place the pot over a high level of heat and fill it with some water.
2. Allow the water to begin boiling before moving to the next step.
3. Once the water is nice and boiling remove it from its heating source. Combine with the hot water your bulgur and place a lid over the pot.
4. Let the bulgur sit for about 20 mins.
5. Now grab a container for mixing, preferably a bowl, and put the bulgur into the container. Combine the following items with the bulgur: mint, salt, parsley, onions, lemon juice, tomatoes, and olive oil.
6. Now you want to toss your bulgur mixture and then place it in the fridge for about one hr (until cool).
7. Plate, and enjoy.

LEBANESE
Garlic Sauce

🥣 Prep Time: 15 mins
🕐 Total Time: 40 mins

Servings per Recipe: 4 cups
Calories	191 kcal
Carbohydrates	3 g
Cholesterol	0 mg
Fat	20.3 g
Fiber	0.2 g
Protein	0.5 g
Sodium	74 mg

Ingredients

4 bulbs garlic, cloves separated and peeled
1 cup lemon juice
1 tsp salt
3 cups olive oil

Directions

1. Okay, to begin lets grab our blender and get it ready for some work.
2. Put the following items into the blender and blend them down until they are nice and smooth: salt, garlic cloves, and juiced lemon. Take care to use a medium blending speed throughout the process.
3. While the contents are being blended you should gradually add some olive oil in a slow but steady stream.
4. Once the mixture becomes thick you should place it into a container with a lid and store it in the fridge.
5. Once cool. Enjoy

Lebanese
Red Lentil Soup

Prep Time: 20 mins
Total Time: 50 mins

Servings per Recipe: 8
Calories	276 kcal
Carbohydrates	39.1 g
Cholesterol	1 mg
Fat	7 g
Fiber	9.1 g
Protein	16.7 g
Sodium	524 mg

Ingredients

6 cups chicken stock

1 lb red lentils

3 tbsps olive oil

1 tbsp minced garlic

1 large onion, chopped

1 tbsp ground cumin

1/2 tsp cayenne pepper

1/2 cup chopped cilantro

3/4 cup fresh lemon juice

Directions

1. Grab a nice sized pan and combine lentils and chicken stock. We want to get the lentils and chicken stock to a boiling state before proceeding.
2. Once the stock is boiling, lower the heating source to medium to low-ish level, and place a lid on the pan.
3. For 20 mins allow the lentils to lightly simmer.
4. Now let the lentils continue to simmer and grab a frying pan or skillet.
5. Place some olive oil in the pan and heat it with a medium to high level of heat.
6. Once the oil is hot combine onions and garlic. Fry these onions and garlic for approx. 3 mins. You will notice the onions become see through.
7. Once the onions and garlic are ready combine them with the lentils.
8. Also combine the lentils with some cayenne and cumin for extra tastiness.
9. Allow the lentils to keep cooking until you find them soft. The lentil cooking process should take ten mins.
10. Now for the final step we need a blender. Prep your blender and puree the soup. The puree can also be done by using a stick or wooden spoon. Make sure your soup is nice and smooth before adding lemon juice and some cilantro.
11. Serve.

LENTIL
Lemon Chard Soup

🍳 Prep Time: 30 mins

🕐 Total Time: 3 hrs 30 mins

Servings per Recipe: 6

Calories	263 kcal
Carbohydrates	41.9 g
Cholesterol	0 mg
Fat	5.5 g
Fiber	18.5 g
Protein	15.7 g
Sodium	263 mg

Ingredients

1 (14.5 ounce) can chicken broth

6 cups water

1 small onion, peeled and diced

1 bay leaf

3 sprigs Italian flat leaf parsley

2 sprigs fresh thyme

4 cups water

1 1/2 cups dried brown lentils, rinsed and drained

1 1/2 lbs Swiss chard - rinsed, stems removed and cut into 1/2 inch slices

2 tbsps olive oil

1 large onion, finely chopped

4 cloves garlic, crushed

3 tbsps chopped fresh cilantro

1/2 cup lemon juice

salt (your preferred amount)

1 lemon, cut into wedges

Directions

1. To make this recipe grab a pan that can be covered later, possibly a saucepan. Inside of the pan let's mix the following ingredients thyme, chicken broth, parsley, six cups water, bay leave, and one onion.

2. Put the contents over a medium to high level of heat, stirring a bit, and let the broth and water begin to boil.

3. Once a boiling state is achieved we want to lower the temperature of the heating source to a medium to low level. Let the broth continue to simmer quietly for about one and a half hours.

4. Once the broth has cooked for about an hour and a half strain it and save four cups for our next steps.

5. Store the remnants for other recipes in the fridge in an air tight container.

6. Grab a large pot for soup, possibly a soup pot if you own one.

7. Combine four cups of water and broth with lentils. Bring the contents to a boiling state. Once everything is boiling, lower the heat to its lowest level and place a lid on the pot. Let

your lentils stew for about one hour.

8. Grab a large frying pan or skillet and heat some olive oil with a medium level of heat.

9. Grab your onion and fry it until translucent. Now you should add some garlic continue frying until you notice a nice fragrance.

10. Finally we want to grab our chards, combine them with the onions and garlic and continue frying for about 5 mins or until you notice the chards are wilted.

11. Combine the chards, onions, and garlic with the lentils and combine also some cilantro, and juiced lemon. You can also add some salt if you like but it is not necessary.

12. Let everything simmer for about 15 mins.

13. Serve, enjoy.

LEBANESE
Chicken Shawarma

 Prep Time: 10 mins
Total Time: 5 hrs

Servings per Recipe: 8

Calories	402 kcal
Carbohydrates	44 g
Cholesterol	58 mg
Fat	15.2 g
Fiber	4 g
Protein	23.3 g
Sodium	420 mg

Ingredients

1/2 cup malt vinegar
1/4 cup plain yogurt
1 tbsp vegetable oil
salt and pepper (your preferred amount)
1 tsp mixed spice
1/4 tsp freshly ground cardamom
8 skinless, boneless chicken thighs
1/2 cup tahini
1/4 cup plain yogurt
1/2 tsp minced garlic

2 tbsps lemon juice
1 tbsp olive oil
1 tbsp chopped fresh parsley
salt and pepper (your preferred amount)
4 medium tomatoes, thinly sliced
1/2 cup sliced onion
4 cups shredded lettuce
8 pita bread rounds

Directions

1. First let's begin by grabbing a nice sized container safe for baking typically something that is glass.
2. Inside of our dish we want to combine the following items: pepper, malt vinegar, salt, one fourth cup of yogurt, cardamom, veggie oil, and mixed spice.
3. Grab your chicken and cover each piece with the seasoning evenly. Once you have covered each piece, evenly take the chicken pieces and place them into a new container and place this container in the fridge for four hrs (overnight is preferred).
4. Now that our chicken pieces have been nice and seasoned let's get our oven ready for some baking.
5. Turn on the oven to 350 degrees Fahrenheit or 175 degrees Celsius.
6. Grab a small container good for mixing (possibly a bowl) combine the following things:

pepper, tahini, salt, one fourth cup of yogurt, parsley, garlic, olive oil, and juiced lemon.

7. Place a lid on the container and put it in the fridge for cooling.

8. Grab your chicken and cover its dish with some foil let everything cook in the oven for about 30 mins. Take care to turn the chicken at least once.

9. After 30 mins has elapsed remove the cover from the baking dish and continue to cook for another five to ten mins. Make sure the chicken is fully cooked through and nice and brown.

10. Take out the chicken from the baking dish and slice it.

11. Place the chicken pieces with some onion, tomato, and lettuce on pieces of pita bread.

12. Cover the chicken with the yogurt based topping and serve.

13. Enjoy.

LEBANESE
Chicken and Potatoes

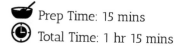 Prep Time: 15 mins

Total Time: 1 hr 15 mins

Servings per Recipe: 6
Calories	592 kcal
Carbohydrates	53.9 g
Cholesterol	65 mg
Fat	30.5 g
Fiber	6.5 g
Protein	26.7 g
Sodium	81 mg

Ingredients

8 cut up chicken pieces
8 medium potatoes, peeled and quartered
salt (your preferred amount)
ground white pepper (your preferred amount)
4 cloves garlic, crushed

1/2 cup extra virgin olive oil
1 cup fresh lemon juice

Directions

1. Start this recipe by heating the oven to 425 degrees Fahrenheit or 220 degrees Celsius.
2. Now grab a nice sized container safe for baking and put your potatoes and chicken in it. You want to now add a good amount of white pepper and salt to the meat.
3. Now grab another container good for mixing, preferably a bowl, and combine the following items: juiced lemon, garlic, and olive oil. Take care to mix everything graciously and coat your meats with this seasoning.
4. Now you should take some aluminum foil and cover the dish containing the meats with it.
5. Place the meats into the oven for about 30 mins.
6. After 30 mins you want to remove the aluminum cover and increase the temperature of the oven to 475 degrees Fahrenheit or 245 degrees Celsius.
7. Continue to allow the potatoes and meat to bake until they are nice and brown and crispy. This should take about 30 more mins.
8. Allow food to cool and plate.
9. Enjoy.

41632883R00058

Printed in Poland
by Amazon Fulfillment
Poland Sp. z o.o., Wrocław